2017

Africa Sustainable Development Report:

Tracking Progress on Agenda 2063 and the Sustainable Development Goals

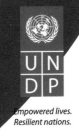

Empowered lives.
Resilient nations.

Ordering information

To order copies of **2017 Africa Sustainable Development Report: Tracking Progress on Agenda 2063 and the Sustainable Development Goals**, please contact:

Publications Section
Economic Commission for Africa
Menelik II Avenue
P.O. Box 3001
Addis Ababa, Ethiopia

Tel: +251 11 544-9900
Fax: +251 11 551-4416
E-mail: ecainfo@uneca.org
Web: www.uneca.org

Sales no.: E.17.II.K.5
ISBN: 978-92-1-125130-2
eISBN: 978-92-1-362743-3

Cover design, layout and graphics: Karen Knols,
Carolina Rodriguez and Tessa Schlechtriem

Printed in Addis Ababa by the ECA Printing and
Publishing Unit. ISO 14001:2004 certified.

Printed on chlorine free paper.

Table of Contents

LISTS OF BOXES, FIGURES & TABLES V

FOREWORD VIII

ACKNOWLEDGEMENTS X

EXECUTIVE SUMMARY XI

CHAPTER 1   INTRODUCTION:
             SCOPE, METHODOLOGY AND STATISTICS IN AFRICA 1

1.1   Scope and methodology 2

1.2   About the report 2

1.3   Statistics in Africa: key issues 3
      1.3.1 Overview of data issues in Africa 3
      1.3.2 Situation of data and statistics in Africa 3

1.4   Statistics for progress reporting on the 2030 Agenda and Agenda 2063 ... 7
      1.4.1 Indicators for the 2030 Agenda and Agenda 2063: Africa's contribution ... 7
      1.4.2 Data availability and opportunities for reporting on Agenda 2063 and the
             2030 Agenda 7
      1.4.3 Africa's contributions to informing the global database of Sustainable Development
             Goal indicators on Africa 9
      1.4.4 Advocacy for action 9

1.5   Conclusion 12

CHAPTER 2   SUSTAINABLE DEVELOPMENT GOAL 1:
             END POVERTY IN ALL ITS FORMS EVERYWHERE 13

1.1   Introduction 14

1.2   Targets and alignment with Agenda 2063 14

1.3   Progress in poverty reduction 14

1.4   Conclusion 26

CHAPTER 3   SUSTAINABLE DEVELOPMENT GOAL 2:
             ZERO HUNGER 27

1.1   Introduction 28

1.2   Targets and alignment with Agenda 2063 28

1.3   Progress and trends regarding the targets 31

1.4   Conclusion 43

CHAPTER 4 SUSTAINABLE DEVELOPMENT GOAL 3:
GOOD HEALTH AND WELL-BEING 45

1.1 Introduction 46

1.2 Targets and alignment with Agenda 2063 46

1.3 Current status in Africa and the progress made 49

1.4 Conclusion 63

CHAPTER 5 SUSTAINABLE DEVELOPMENT GOAL 5:
GENDER EQUALITY 65

1.1 Introduction 66

1.2 Targets and alignment with Agenda 2063. 66

1.3 Synergies between the 2030 Agenda, Agenda 2063 and
the Beijing Declaration and Platform for Action 69

1.4 Current status and progress 70

1.5 Conclusion 79

CHAPTER 6 GOAL 9:
INDUSTRY, INNOVATION AND INFRASTRUCTURE 81

1.1 Introduction 82

1.2 Targets and alignment with Agenda 2063 82

1.3 Data availability, current status in Africa and the progress made . . 85

1.4 Conclusion 93

CHAPTER 7 SUSTAINABLE DEVELOPMENT GOAL 14:
LIFE BELOW WATER 95

1.1 Introduction 96

1.2 Targets and alignment with Agenda 2063 98

1.3 Data availability, current status in Africa and the progress made . . 99

1.4 Implications for small island developing States 102

1.5 Conclusion 104

CHAPTER 8 CONCLUSION AND RECOMMENDATIONS 105

1.1 Conclusion 106

1.2 Recommendations 107

REFERENCES 109

List of boxes, figures & tables

List of boxes

Box 2.1   Global poverty: overview 16

Box 3.1   Global hunger: most recent overview 31

Box 3.2   El Niño effects threaten Africa's food security 32

Box 4.1   Global health status: most recent overview 48

Box 6.1   Key facts in industry, innovation and infrastructure globally ... 85

Box 6.2   Promotion of renewable energy in Morocco 90

Box 7.1   Key facts about life below water for Africa 99

Box 7.2   Small island developing States environmental issues: lessons from Seychelles 103

List of figures

Figure 1.1   Milestones in the development of statistics in Africa 4

Figure 2.1   Subregional trends in GDP growth and Annual GDP growth by Region, 2010–2015 16

Figure 2.2   GDP growth rates, 2005-2014 18

Figure 2.3   Proportion of people living below $1.90/day, 2002-2013 19

Figure 2.4   Changes in poverty rates, 2002-2012 19

Figure 2.5   Proportion of working population living under $1.90 per day 20

Figure 2.6   Vulnerable employment per region 21

Figure 2.7   Proportion of workers living below the poverty line by age 22

Figure 2.8   Gender distribution of the total working poor by region 23

Figure 2.9   Proportion of employed population below the poverty line by sex ... 23

Figure 2.10 Proportion of unemployed receiving unemployment benefits 24

Figure 2.11 Social assistance, social insurance and labour market programme coverage, 2000-2014 25

Figure 3.1   Estimated prevalence of moderate or severe food insecurity in the adult population 34

Figure 3.2   Children under 5 years of age with WHZ<-2, 2014 35

Figure 3.3   Agricultural irrigated land as percentage of total agricultural land ... 37

Figure 3.4   Annual agriculture share in total public expenditure 40

Figure 4.1   Maternal mortality ratio by country in 2013 and 2015 51

Figure 4.2   Proportion of births attended by skilled health personnel per region ... 52

Figure 4.3   Proportion of births attended by skilled health personnel in African countries ... 53

Figure 4.4   Under-five mortality rate by region 54

Figure 4.5   Under-five mortality rate by country, 2013 and 2015 55

Figure 4.6   Neonatal mortality rate by region 56

Figure 4.7   Neonatal mortality rate by country 57

Figure 4.8   Estimated HIV incidence rate by gender, 2015 59

Figure 4.9   Death rate due to road traffic injuries 60

Figure 4.10   Married women or those in a union of reproductive age (between 15 and 49 years)
              who have their need for family planning satisfied with modern methods,
              by region 61

Figure 4.11   Adolescent birth rate among women aged 15 and 19 years by region, 2000 and 2015 . 62

Figure 5.1   Synergies between the Beijing Declaration and Platform for Action,
              Agenda 2063 and the 2030 Agenda 69

Figure 5.2   Adoption of gender-equal laws by African (excluding North African) countries
              by score on legal index 70

Figure 5.3   Women subjected to physical/sexual violence in selected countries 71

Figure 5.4   Proportion of women between 20 and 24 years of age who were married
              by 18 years of age 73

Figure 5.5   Early marriage in Africa 74

Figure 5.6   Proportion of girls between the 15 and 19 years of age who have undergone
              female genital mutilation/circumcision 74

Figure 5.7   Proportion of women in national parliaments, 2016 76

Figure 5.8   Proportion people with an account at a financial institution in
              Africa (excluding North Africa) 77

Figure 5.9   Mobile account ownership in Africa (excluding North Africa) 78

Figure 6.1   Air transport, passengers carried 86

Figure 6.2   Air transport, freight 87

Figure 6.3   Donors to Africa's infrastructure, 2008-2010 92

Figure 7.1   Coverage of protected areas in relation to marine areas, by region (2014) 101

Figure 7.2   Coverage of protected areas, 2016 102

List of tables

Table 1.1   Sustainable Development Goal data availability on African countries 8

Table 1.2   Data sources of Sustainable Development Goal indicators on Africa 9

Table 2.1   Alignment of Sustainable Development Goal 1 of the 2030 Agenda
with that of Agenda 2063 15

Table 3.1   Alignment of Sustainable Development Goal 2 of the 2030 Agenda
with that of Agenda 2063 29

Table 3.2   Global prevalence of undernourishment by region (PER CENT) 33

Table 3.3   Children under 5 years of age with HAZ <-2, by Region* (PER CENT) 35

Table 3.4   Agricultural value added per worker (CONSTANT 2010 UNITED STATES DOLLARS) 37

Table 3.5   Level of risk of extinction of local breeds, by region (PER CENT) 38

Table 3.6   Agriculture orientation index of government expenditure* 39

Table 3.7   Total official disbursements for agriculture
(BILLIONS OF CONSTANT 2014 UNITED STATES DOLLARS) 41

Table 3.8   Producer support estimate (BILLIONS OF UNITED STATES DOLLARS) 41

Table 3.9   Agricultural export subsidies (BILLIONS OF UNITED STATES DOLLARS) 42

Table 4.1   Alignment of Sustainable Development Goal 3 of the 2030 Agenda
with that of Agenda 2063 47

Table 4.2   Maternal mortality ratio by region (DEATHS PER 100,000 LIVE BIRTHS) 49

Table 4.3   Estimated HIV incidence rate by region
(NUMBER OF NEW INFECTIONS PER 1,000 UNINFECTED PEOPLE) 58

Table 4.4   Alcohol consumption by region (LITRES OF PURE ALCOHOL CONSUMED PER CAPITA) 58

Table 5.1   Alignment of Sustainable Development Goal 5 of the 2030 Agenda
with that of Agenda 2063 67

Table 6.1   Alignment of Sustainable Development Goal 9 of the 2030 Agenda
with that of Agenda 2063 83

Table 6.2   Manufacturing value added per capita (CONSTANT 2010 UNITED STATES DOLLARS) 89

Table 6.3   Manufacturing employment as a proportion of total employment (PER CENT) 89

Table 7.1   Alignment of Sustainable Development Goal 14 of the 2030 Agenda
with that of Agenda 2063 96

Table 7.2   Indicators of Sustainable Development Goal 14 by tier of data availability
and methodology definition 100

Foreword

The 2017 Africa regional report on Agenda 2063 and the Sustainable Development Goals (SDGs) assesses the continent's performance in domesticating and implementing the two development frameworks since their adoption in 2013 and 2015, respectively. The report is aligned with the theme of the 2017 High Level Political Forum on Sustainable Development (HLPF): "Eradicating poverty and promoting prosperity in a changing world". It focuses on the following six goals of the HLPF: Goal 1 (End Poverty); Goal 2 – (Zero Hunger); Goal 3 (Good Health and Well-being); Goal 5 (Gender Equality); Goal 9 (Industry, Innovation and Infrastructure); and Goal 14 (Life below water).

A critical contribution of this report is that it provides a baseline for performance tracking going forward. However, the scope and depth of analysis of the report is framed by the availability of data which is weak, particularly on indicators pertaining to environmental sustainability, and the progress on democratic and electoral governance, human rights and rule of law.

Approximately six out of every ten SDG indicators cannot be tracked in Africa due to severe data limitations. Strengthening statistical systems in Africa is an imperative for successful implementation of the SDGs and Agenda 2063 as it underpins evidence based policy making. Disaggregated data by age, gender, income and geographical location is necessary to better target support to groups at risk of being left behind in the development process.

The report is the first to simultaneously track progress on the 2030 Agenda for Sustainable development and Agenda 2063 (and its first ten-year implementation plan). This is possible due to the substantial convergence at the level of goals, targets and indicators. This is illustrated by a mapping of the links between the global and continental initiatives included at the beginning of each chapter.

The report underscores the slow progress towards poverty reduction in Africa despite the accelerated growth enjoyed over the past decade. Noting the disproportionate prevalence of poverty among women and youth, the report highlights the lack of inclusiveness and sustainability of primary-commodity driven growth and reiterates the call for structural transformation anchored by commodity-based industrialization and accelerated reduction in inequality.

The report observes that Africa's infrastructure deficits undermine industrial development and underline the stagnation in value addition in manufacturing. And, even though value-addition in agriculture has been rising, it remains substantially low by global standards due, in part to limited investments and inefficiencies at all levels of the agricultural production chain. Increased efficiency of investments in agriculture, both private and public, is vital to addressing food insecurity in Africa. Land reforms to ensure that women have more ownership to this important resource and expanding irrigation from the current five percent are critical to improving agricultural productivity and total output.

Improving the productive capacities of the labor force requires investing in skills and health of all segments of the population regardless of gender. The report underlines improvements in gender parity in enrollments at the primary and secondary school levels. It also notes significant improvements in women's representation in national parliaments. Improvements in health systems are also manifested by substantial declines in maternal and child deaths as a result of improved access to skilled birth attendants, reduced adolescent fertility rates and increased access to family planning. Yet the levels of child and maternal deaths remain unacceptably high and constitute a drain on the continent's human resources.

The dramatic increase in access to mobile telephone networks documented in the report constitutes a unique opportunity to strengthen financial inclusion in Africa. Indeed, technological innovations, such as MPesa that facilitate the use of mobile telephones for financial transactions have made it possible for the under-served and unbanked segments of society to gain access to financial services including mobile accounts. Ultimately this trend could spur entrepreneurship among vulnerable groups and promote inclusive and sustainable growth.

Finally, the report looks at the issue of sustainable use of oceans, seas and marine resources for economic and social development that meets the needs of the present without compromising the ability of future generations to meet their own needs. While oceans and seas play a critical role in economic activity and regulating the global climate, African coastal and island states are threatened by increased environmental degradation and the risk of flooding. Globally, sustainable levels of fish stocks declined from 70.1 to 68.6 per cent between 2009-2013 owing to overfishing, illegal and unregulated fishing and destructive fishing practices. Thirty-eight African states are now taking steps towards better management of life below water.

Successful implementation of the SDGs and Agenda 2063 will require an integrated approach that coordinates the efforts of all sectors of government working in collaboration with the private sector and civil society. We are hopeful that the insights and data contained in this report will be a useful guide for policymakers.

Moussa Faki Mahamat	**Vera Songwe**	**Akinwumi A. Adesina**	**Achim Steiner**
Chair Person	Executive Secretary	President	Administrator
African Union Commission	United Nations Economic Commission for Africa	African Development Bank Group	United Nations Development Programme

Acknowledgements

This report is a joint annual publication of the African Union Commission (AUC), the Economic Commission for Africa (ECA) of the United Nations, the African Development Bank (AfDB) and the United Nations Development Programme-Regional Bureau for Africa (UNDP-RBA).

The report was prepared under the overall direction of Moussa Faki Mahamat, AUC Chairperson; Abdalla Hamdok, United Nations Under-Secretary-General and ECA Executive Secretary, a.i.; Akinwumi A. Adesina, AfDB President; and Achim Steiner, UNDP Administrator. Technical guidance was provided by Adam B. Elhiraika, Director, Macroeconomic Policy Division, ECA; Anthony Mothae Maruping, Commissioner for Economic Affairs, AUC; René N'Guettia Kouassi, Director, Economic Affairs Department, AUC; Oley Dibba-Wadda, Director, Human Capital, Youth and Skills Development Department, AfDB; Abdoulaye Mar Dieye, Assistant Administrator and Regional Director, UNDP-RBA; and Ayodele Odusola, Chief Economist and Head of Strategy and Analysis Team, UNDP-RBA.

Preparation of the report was coordinated by a core team led by Bartholomew Armah, Chief, Renewal of Planning Section, Macroeconomic Policy Division, ECA; Selamawit Mussie (Policy Officer, AUC); Mona Sharan (Gender Specialist, AfDB) and Eunice Kamwendo (Strategic Advisor, UNDP). Chapters of the report were drafted by the following lead authors: Negussie Gorfe, ECA (Chapter 1 – Statistics in Africa); Eunice Kamwendo, UNDP (Chapter 2 - Ending Poverty); Amarakoon Bandara, UNDP (Chapter 3 – Zero Hunger); Selamawit Mussie, AUC (Chapter 4 – Good Health); Mona Sharan, AfDB (Chapter 5 – Gender Equality); Mama Keita, ECA (Chapter 6 – Industry, innovation and infrastructure); and Paul Mpuga, ECA (Chapter 7 – Life below water & Chapter 8 – Recommendations).

Technical contributions from the following are highly appreciated: Leila Ben Ali, AUC; Robert Ndieka, AUC; Charles Wangadya, AUC; Kassim M. Khamis, AUC; Dossina Yeo, AUC; Ngone Diop, ECA; Fatouma Sissoko, ECA; Eskedar Abebe, ECA; Seung Jin Baek[1], ESCWA; Osten Chulu, UNDP; Luka Okumu, UNDP; Colleen Zamba, UNDP; Roland Alcindor, UNDP; Dr. Ojebiyi Olusegun, Ladoke Akintola University of Technology, Nigeria.

The report benefitted from wide-ranging consultations with stakeholders and policymakers. Stakeholders included African government representatives, academia, and civil society. The consultations included an Expert Group Meeting to validate the draft report, held from 29th May to 1 June 2017 in Mahe, Seychelles. Participants included the Agenda 2063/ SDGs focal persons from African countries as well as representatives from civil society organizations and the United Nations agencies.

The report benefitted from editorial, translation, graphic design, printing, media and communications and secretarial support from Demba Diarra, Teshome Yohannes, Charles Ndungu, Kokebe George, Yechi Bekele, Marille Benoit, Preethi Sushil, SeproTech Multilingual Solutions, and Melanie Guedenet.

---

1   Formerly at ECA.

Executive Summary

The 2017 edition of the Africa Sustainable Development report on Agenda 2063 and the 2030 Agenda uses the latest harmonized data to assess the continent's performance with regard to implementing both Agendas, identify opportunities and challenges and recommend actions to hasten progress. Documenting the progress made and the lessons learned in the implementation of both Agendas can be useful in strengthening efforts going forward.

The report is aligned with the following six Sustainable Development Goals of the 2017 high-level political forum on sustainable development: Goal 1 (No poverty); Goal 2 (Zero hunger); Goal 3 (Good health and well-being); Goal 5 (Gender equality); Goal 9 (Industry, innovation and infrastructure); and Goal 14 (Life below water). The key messages and findings regarding these six Goals and data issues are summarized below. Progress on the other Goals will be discussed in future reports.

1 Slow progress made in reducing poverty and inequality owing to limited decent employment opportunities and weak social insurance mechanisms

The rate of decline in extreme poverty ($1.90 per day) has been slow in Africa, declining a mere 15 per cent during the period 1990-2013. Women and young people bear the brunt of poverty. Decent jobs, which are an important route out of poverty, are hard to find because Africa's growth has not created sufficient jobs to match demand. Approximately 60 per cent of jobs in Africa are considered vulnerable. Less than 1 per cent of the unemployed receive unemployment benefits and only 19 per cent of the African (excluding North African) population is covered by social insurance. The lack of decent  jobs, coupled with weak social insurance schemes, have, in turn, contributed to high rates of poverty among the working population. Notwithstanding a decline in the prevalence of the working poor in Africa (excluding North Africa), one of every three workers lived in extreme poverty in 2015. Working young people and women are disproportionately affected by the burden of poverty. In 2015, 32.1 per cent of working men, compared with 35.1 per cent of working women, were classified as poor.

2 Rising food insecurity and undernourishment are a growing concern in Africa (excluding North Africa)

 Some 355 million people in Africa were moderately or severely food insecure in 2015. Although food insecurity declined in North Africa, from 7.7 per cent in 2014 to 6.4 per cent in 2016, in Africa (excluding North Africa), severe food insecurity increased from 25.3 per cent to 26.1 per cent during the same period. Food insecurity is invariably undermining efforts to address undernourishment. Some 217 million people were undernourished during the period 2014–2016, an increase of 6 per cent compared with 2010–2012. This was largely the result of low agricultural productivity and high population growth rates.

3 Agricultural value added is rising but low, due in part to limited irrigation coverage and declining investment in the sector

Improving agricultural productivity is vital to addressing food insecurity in Africa. Measured in terms of agricultural value added, Africa's agricultural productivity is on the rise but remains well below the global average. Agricultural value added increased 9 per cent during the period 2010-2015 but was only 62 per cent of the world average in 2015. Binding constraints to agricultural productivity in Africa include limited irrigation infrastructure and low budgetary allocations to the sector. Only 5 per cent of agricultural land in Africa is irrigated, compared with 41 per cent in Asia and 21 per cent globally. Furthermore, fiscal allocations to the sector are well below the 10 per cent of budgetary resources committed in the Maputo Protocol. Globally, support for agricultural producers more than doubled, from $258 billion in 2000 to $584 million in 2014.

4 Gender disparities in education and national parliaments are declining, but conservative norms and practices are holding back progress

Gender disparities have narrowed at the primary and secondary school levels, but progress remains slow, in particular at the tertiary level. Gender parity in primary school increased from 86 per cent in 1990 to 96 per cent in 2013, while parity in secondary schools rose from 71 per cent to 90 per cent during the same period. On the other hand, parity at tertiary levels remains low. Nevertheless, the continent has made significant progress in increasing the representation of women in national parliaments; this figure increased 14 percentage points (from 8 to 22 per cent) during the period 1990-2015.

Furthermore, more women are seeking employment in the formal and informal sectors; however, limited education, conservative norms and traditions that relegate women to unpaid house work, for example, constitute obstacles to women's empowerment.

Conservative norms such as child marriages can truncate women's careers and thereby limit the full realization of their productive capacities. While child marriages have been declining, they remain high, in particular in Africa (excluding North Africa), where 37 per cent of women between the ages of 20 and 24 were married by age 18.

Harmful traditional practices, such female genital mutilation, constitute a form of discrimination against women. Notwithstanding substantial progress, female genital mutilation is particularly high in North Africa, where an estimated 70 per cent of girls between the ages of 15 and 19 years of age were subjected to the procedure in 2015.

Meanwhile, women continue to be victims of violence, both in the household and in public spaces. Violence against women is especially severe in conflict-affected settings and during periods of war.

Cultures and traditions that inhibit women from fully participating in education, economic activities and social life need to be addressed. Keeping girls and boys in school can promote and sustain gender equality by breaking cycles of ignorance, poverty and stereotypes.

5 Measures aimed at improving access to contraceptives and skilled birth attendants have reduced adolescent births and child and maternal deaths

There have been significant gains in health in the past decade, including a substantial decline in child and maternal mortality. However, the continent still has the highest burden of maternal and child deaths compared with other regions globally. Maternal mortality rates in Africa (excluding North Africa) dropped 35 per cent during the period 2000-2015, while North Africa has already met the target of 70 maternal deaths per 100,000 live births. Similar declines are observed for under-five deaths (46 per cent) and neonatal (30 per cent) deaths during the same period. These positive trends are attributable in part to improved access to skilled birth attendants and family planning. Both interventions may have contributed to the 21 per cent decline in adolescent birth rates observed during the period 2000-2015. The continent has also significantly curbed the incidence of HIV, which declined 62 per cent during the same period. Nevertheless, the averages mask significant subregional and country disparities, and Africa is home to the highest HIV incidence rate globally.

6 Enforcing road safety regulations mediates the impact of alcohol consumption on deaths due to road traffic injuries.

Alcohol consumption has been linked to the incidence of road traffic-related deaths and injuries. Overall, per capita consumption of pure alcohol in developed regions is almost double the quantity consumed in developing regions. However, consumption has been falling in developed regions and rising in developing regions. In Africa, consumption declined in North Africa, but rose slightly in the rest of the continent, from 6.2 to 6.3 (2005-2015) litres per capita, equalling the global

consumption level. Notwithstanding their higher levels of alcohol consumption, developed regions have the lowest (8.6 percent) death rate due to road traffic injuries. On the other hand, Africa, excluding North Africa, has the highest rate of road traffic-related deaths (26.6 per cent), much higher than the global average (17.4 per cent) in 2013. This trend underlines the effective role that measures aimed at enforcing road safety regulations can play in mediating the impact of excessive alcohol consumption on road traffic-related deaths.

7 Weak infrastructure and limited manufacturing value addition are undermining overall job growth

Access to quality infrastructure is an important prerequisite for industrial development. Infrastructure connects producers to markets in an efficient manner and thereby reduces production and distribution costs, increases competitiveness, attracts new investors and fosters economic growth. Owing to data restrictions, the report largely focuses on air and rail transport infrastructure.

Air freight and air travel remain extremely low in Africa, excluding North Africa, notwithstanding a rising trend. In 2015, Africa, excluding North Africa, represented 1.3 per cent and 1.5 per cent of the world air travel and air shipping, respectively. However, there has been substantial progress during the past decade and a half. Air freight and air travel increased 34 per cent and 18 per cent, respectively, during the period 2010-2015.

Rail transportation has been instrumental in promoting industrialization in advanced and emerging countries and could do the same in Africa. However, like air transport, rail transportation is still not very well developed in Africa: it accounted for 6 per cent of the total rail in the world, compared with 12 per cent for Asia and the Pacific and 10 per cent for Latin America and the Caribbean.

Weak infrastructure has adverse consequences for manufacturing sector growth. In Africa, excluding North Africa, manufacturing value added stagnated at 10.3 to 10.5 per cent of gross domestic product (GDP) during the period 2010-2015. The corresponding figures for North Africa were 11.2 and 11.5 per cent, respectively. Furthermore, manufacturing value added in Africa tends to be low tech. Medium-tech and high-tech industry value added account for a mere 0.1 per cent of total value added for all African countries with data, compared with approximately 0.5 per cent for the developed countries.

The relatively low share of manufacturing value added in Africa, excluding North Africa, accounted for a 3.57 per cent fall in the sector's contribution to total employment during the 2010-2015 period.

8 Limited investment in research and development obstructs prospects for innovation and technology development

Advances in scientific and technological knowledge through research are critical to eradicating poverty and promoting home-grown solutions to economic and social development challenges.

Currently, Africa as a region spends less than 0.5 per cent of its GDP on research and development, compared with more than 1 per cent in the developing region as a whole and 2 per cent in the developed regions. Research and development expenditure as a share of GDP stagnated at 0.4 per cent during the period 2000-2013 in Africa (excluding the North). On the other hand, North Africa experienced an increase from 0.28 to 0.51 during the same period.

9 Significant increases in the coverage of mobile cellular services is an opportunity for social and financial inclusion

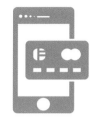

Reliable access to broadband Internet is a key driver of economic growth, job creation and social inclusion. In addition, it facilitates a transition to knowledge-intensive economies by enhancing access to information. The proportion of the population covered by 3G mobile networks in Africa increased significantly, from 25 to 65 per cent during the 2010-2015 period. This trend has enhanced financial inclusion by facilitating virtual access to financial services by previously unbanked segments of society.

10 Globally, the proportion of fish stocks that are at biologically sustainable levels is declining

The world's oceans and seas play a critical role in supporting populations, economic activity and regulating the global climate. Environmental degradation and the risk of flooding are the main challenges to the oceans and coastal areas, respectively. At least 38 African countries are coastal States, 6 of which are island States and thus have a keen interest in better management of life below water.

Globally, sustainable levels of fish stocks declined from 70.1 to 68.6 per cent during the 2009-2013 period owing to overfishing, illegal and unregulated fishing and destructive fishing practices. Subsidies to the fishing industry induce overfishing and adversely affect the ocean food chain, which can lead to food insecurity and poor livelihoods.

Africa's Development Agendas Side By Side

AGENDA 2030 GOAL	AGENDA 2063 GOALS

1 NO POVERTY

1. A high standard of living, quality of life and well-being for all
5. Modern agriculture for increased productivity and production
7. Environmentally sustainable climate resilient economies and communities
17. Full gender equality in all spheres of life

2 ZERO HUNGER

1. A high standard of living, quality of life and well-being for all
3. Healthy and well-nourished citizens
4. Transformed economies and job creation
5. Modern agriculture for increased productivity and production
7. Environmentally sustainable climate resilient economies and communities
8. United Africa (Federal or Confederate)

3 GOOD HEALTH AND WELL-BEING

3. Healthy and well-nourished citizens
7. Environmentally sustainable climate resilient economies and communities
17. Full gender equality in all spheres of life

4 QUALITY EDUCATION

1. A high standard of living, quality of life and well-being for all
2. Well educated citizens and skills revolution underpinned by science, technology and innovation
16. African cultural renaissance is pre-eminent
17. Full gender equality in all spheres of life
18. Engaged and empowered youth and children

5 GENDER EQUALITY

3. Healthy and well-nourished citizens
5. Modern agriculture for increased productivity and production
10. World class infrastructure crisscrosses Africa
17. Full gender equality in all spheres of life

6 CLEAN WATER AND SANITATION

1. A high standard of living, quality of life and well-being for all
7. Environmentally sustainable climate resilient economies and communities

7 AFFORDABLE AND CLEAN ENERGY

1. A high standard of living, quality of life and well-being for all
6. Blue/ ocean economy for accelerated economic growth
7. Environmentally sustainable climate resilient economies and communities
10. World class infrastructure crisscrosses Africa

8 DECENT WORK AND ECONOMIC GROWTH

1. A high standard of living, quality of life and well-being for all
2. Transformed economies and job creation
12. Capable institutions and transformed leadership in place at all levels
16. African cultural renaissance is pre-eminent
17. Full gender equality in all spheres of life
18. Engaged and empowered youth and children

9 INDUSTRY, INNOVATION AND INFRASTRUCTURE

1. A high standard of living, quality of life and well-being for all
4. Transformed economies and job creation
5. Modern agriculture for increased productivity and production
6. Blue/ ocean economy for accelerated economic growth
8. United Africa (federal or confederate)
10. World class infrastructure crisscrosses Africa
19. Africa as a major partner in global affairs and peaceful co-existence

10 REDUCED INEQUALITIES

1. A high standard of living, quality of life and well-being for all
8. United Africa (federal or confederate)
16. African cultural renaissance is pre-eminent
20. Africa takes full responsibility for financing her development

11 SUSTAINABLE CITIES AND COMMUNITIES

1. A high standard of living, quality of life and well-being for all
7. Environmentally sustainable climate resilient economies and communities
10. World class infrastructure crisscrosses Africa
12. Capable institutions and transformed leadership in place at all levels
16. African cultural renaissance is pre-eminent

12 RESPONSIBLE CONSUMPTION AND PRODUCTION

1. A high standard of living, quality of life and well-being for all
4. Transformed economies and job creation
5. Modern agriculture for increased productivity and production
7. Environmentally sustainable climate resilient economies and communities
12. Capable institutions and transformed leadership in place at all levels
16. African cultural renaissance is pre-eminent

13 CLIMATE ACTION

5. Modern agriculture for increased productivity and production
7. Environmentally sustainable climate resilient economies and communities
12. Capable institutions and transformed leadership in place at all levels

14 LIFE BELOW WATER

4. Transformed economies and job creation
6. Blue/ ocean economy for accelerated economic growth
7. Environmentally sustainable climate resilient economies and communities

15 LIFE ON LAND

7. Environmentally sustainable climate resilient economies and communities

16 PEACE, JUSTICE AND STRONG INSTITUTIONS

11. Democratic values, practices, universal principles of human rights, justice and the rule of law entrenched
12. Capable institutions and transformed leadership in place at all levels
13. Peace, security and stability are preserve
17. Full gender equality in all spheres of life
18. Engaged and empowered youth and children

17 PARTNERSHIPS FOR THE GOALS

1. A high standard of living, quality of life and well-being for all
4. Transformed economies and job creation
10. World class infrastructure crisscrosses Africa
12. Capable institutions and transformed leadership in place at all levels
19. Africa as a major partner in global affairs and peaceful co-existence
20. Africa takes full responsibility for financing her development

CHAPTER 1

Introduction:
scope, methodology
and statistics in Africa

1.1 Scope and methodology

The 2017 edition of the Africa regional report on the 2030 Agenda and Agenda 2063 documents the progress made, lessons learned and challenges regarding their adaptation and implementation. The report is informed mainly by latest data from a broad range of sources, including the International Labour Organisation, the United Nations Conference on Trade and Development, the Statistics Division of the United Nations and the World Bank's world development indicators. These are complemented by a review of the latest literature on both Agendas and other pertinent analytical works, especially regarding the goals for which data availability is limited.

The report covers all African countries, with relevant data on Agenda 2063 and the 2030 Agenda regarding the three dimensions of sustainable development (economic, social and environment) and governance and the means of implementation.

To the extent possible, the report disaggregates data by age, gender, geography (regarding the five regions of the continent: Central, East, North, West and Southern Africa) in all the sections. Where data permit, Africa's performance is compared with other regions of the world.

1.2 About the report

The report underscores country performance on the selected goals, targets and indicators of the 2030 Agenda and Agenda 2063. Given the absence of an agreed baseline for both Agendas, 2013 is adopted as the baseline because it represents the most recent year with data on most of the indicators. Given that there are no agreed baselines to date and the fact that many African countries are yet to put in place structures and systems for implementing, monitoring and reporting on the Agendas, this is an area for further discussion. Statistics-related challenges associated with reporting on the Sustainable Development Goals need to be identified. As an annual report, it builds on earlier ones and especially the *MDGs to Agenda 2063/SDGs Transition Report 2016*. In the analysis, the report illustrates the alignment between targets and indicators of the goals contained in the 2030 Agenda and Agenda 2063.

The report is prepared jointly by the staffs of the African Development Bank (AfDB), the African Union Commission, the Economic Commission for Africa (ECA) and the United Nations Development Programme's (UNDP) Regional Bureau for Africa. Teams were responsible for writing specific chapters. Given the large number of Sustainable Development Goals and indicators, the report is aligned with the theme of the high-level political forum and focuses on the corresponding goals for 2017, which include Goal 1 (No poverty), Goal 2 (Zero hunger), Goal 3 (Good health and well-being), Goal 5 (Gender equality), Goal 9 (Industry, innovation and infrastructure) and Goal 14 (Life below water).

The introductory chapter underscores the approach to the preparation of the report. It outlines the availability and state of data and statistics, as well as areas for strengthening to generate baselines on key indicators and ensure adequate reporting over time. This is followed by chapter two, which focuses on progress on ending poverty (Goal 1). Chapter three highlights progress and issues regarding ending hunger (Goal 2) and chapter four focuses on progress on ensuring healthy lives (Goal 3). In chapter five, the report underscores progress on gender equality (Goal 5), followed by chapter six on resilient infrastructure and industrialization (Goal 9). Chapter seven focuses on progress on and issues relating to life below water (Goal 14). Lastly, chapter eight concludes with policy recommendations.

1.3 Statistics in Africa: key issues

1.3.1 Overview of data issues in Africa

The Sustainable Development Goals have rekindled interest in the quality and availability of statistics for management, programme design and the monitoring and evaluation of performance. It is estimated that some $1 billion annually is required to enable 77 of the world's lower-income countries to establish statistical systems capable of supporting and measuring the Goals. Existing mechanisms, such as multilateral lending, bilateral grants and technical assistance, ought to be used to support statistics. Equally, multilateral trust funds and special development grants ought to cover the financial gap in developing statistics for the Goals.

African development statistics are as varied as the continent itself and the herculean task has always been to bring all actors into a continental framework for statistical development. In October 2014, the Independent Expert Advisory Group on Data Revolution for Sustainable Development underscored the opportunities and challenges confronting statistical production for sustainable development. It was clearly stated that investment is required to improve statistics for the effective measurement of sustainable development indicators (Independent Expert Advisory Group on the Data Revolution for Sustainable Development, 2014). Equally, the monitoring and evaluation of the Goals will require additional investment in order to consolidate gains made during the Millennium Development Goal period, enabling the development of reliable, high-quality data on a range of subjects, including but not limited to climate change and inequalities. As a result, the African national statistical system and subregional and regional organizations dealing with statistics and statistical development have been not only challenged, but also given the opportunity, among other things, to raise public awareness of the importance of statistics in the development of the continent and in harnessing national, subregional, regional and international resources in building the capacities of African countries to meet the increased demand in quality statistics emanating from their development agendas.

The recent upsurge in the demand for statistics in Africa is driven, among other factors, by the global recession of 2008 and the search for data for investment oppor-

African developmental statistics is under transformation and inadequate funding to sustain statistical development and track the right indicators for decision-making remains a core problem.

tunities in the continent. The emerging capital markets and stock exchanges require quality data on inflation, gross domestic product (GDP) and other economic data for appropriate investment decisions, to some extent explaining the pressure exerted on national statistical offices. Domestic requirements for good governance and accountability as a tool for evaluating government performance has increased demand for data. Donors also exert demand for data, especially on social trends to enable them to be held accountable to their constituents, leading to donor-driven data generation that is sometimes irrelevant to Africa's development (Kiregyera, 2015). The problem is aggravated by the underfunding of national statistical offices and a reliance on donors, in particular for household surveys and censuses. This calls for increased investment in both economic and social data.

1.3.2 Situation of data and statistics in Africa

It is noted by development practitioners and other actors that deficiencies in statistical information hamper Africa's development and transformation processes. Although some progress had been made in statistical development, this progress is uneven and the national statistical systems still face a number of challenges. In response to concerns raised by stakeholders in the national statistical systems in various forums, a number of initiatives, frameworks and strategies have been developed in the past decades to improve statistics in support of Africa's development agenda (Economic Commission for Africa, 2008; 2013). FIGURE 1.1 highlights the key milestones in the development of statis-

AFRICA SUSTAINABLE DEVELOPMENT REPORT 2017

FIGURE I.I   MILESTONES IN THE DEVELOPMENT OF STATISTICS IN AFRICA

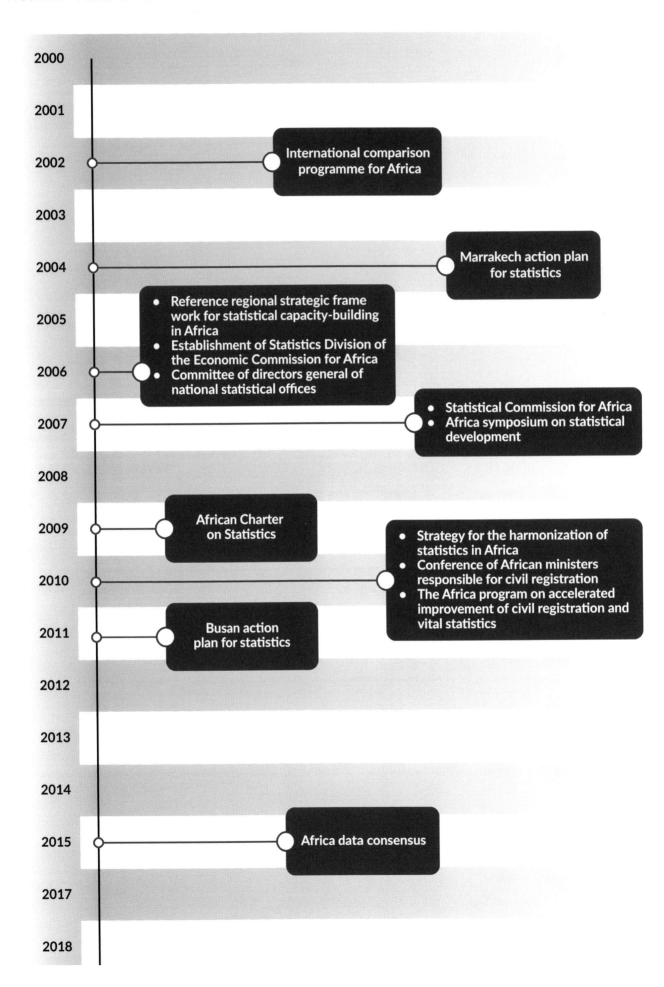

tics in Africa. These deliberate efforts need to be put into concrete action at the country and regional levels in order to develop data systems on the continent.

Those initiatives, together with the efforts to measure progress on achieving the Millennium Development Goals, led to increased investment in a number of national statistics systems (Economic Commission for Africa, 2016) and contributed to improvements in data availability. They have also contributed to significant capacity development in the region. The main challenges to statistical development in Africa are discussed in the paragraphs that follow.

i Inadequate funding and limited autonomy of the national statistical offices

Adequate and sustained resourcing and autonomy of the national statistics system, in particular the national statistical offices, are key determinants of the production of accurate, credible, timely and neutral data. African developmental statistics is under transformation and inadequate funding to sustain statistical development and track the right indicators for decision-making remains a core problem. The lack of institutional and political autonomy has also weakened the technical and managerial capacity of many offices to deliver effectively. Of the 54 African countries, only 12 are considered to have autonomous offices (Economic Commission for Africa, 2010).

These shortfalls contribute to capacity limits that have resulted in inadequate access to and use of data, an inability to use the latest statistical methodologies, and a statistical knowledge gap in issues such as metadata flow, updating statistical data and the timely production of quality data to monitor and evaluate national continental and global development agendas. Several countries in Africa are working towards granting their national statistical offices autonomy through legal and institutional reforms. However, progress is uneven among countries.

ii Data availability

There is improvement in data availability in African countries following increased implementation of censuses and household surveys and the use of technology in these processes. The unprecedented participation of African countries in the 2010 round of the population and housing census is an illustration of this improvement. During that round, 47 countries conducted population censuses, compared with 38 countries for the 2000 round and 44 countries for the 1990 round (Economic Commission for Africa and African Union Commission, 2014). Notwithstanding this progress, most countries are not able to collect data in a regular and timely manner, in particular conflict and post-conflict countries. The gaps in regular data production are underscored by the Mo Ibrahim Foundation (2016): only half of Africa's population live in a country that has conducted more than two comparable surveys in the past 10 years and a little more than half live in a country that has conducted an agriculture census in the past 10 years or one that has not conducted a labour force survey. In addition, improvements in other data sources, such as administrative data, civil registration and vital statistics and geospatial data, have been very slow (Organization for Economic Cooperation and Development and Paris21, 2013).

These limitations lead to persistent data gaps in key development indicators, such as social, environmental and governance indicators (Cassidy, 2014), administrative data (including civil registration and vital statistics and data on industry and drug usage) and indicators on the structure of the agriculture sector and landholders and on labour market and employment (Mo Ibrahim Foundation, 2016). The data gaps impede the establishment of baselines for measuring progress on development frameworks, including the Sustainable Development Goals. Data limitations compound the challenge relating to monitoring the Goals. On the basis of the global database on the Goals, updated on 4 January 2017, only 37.8 per cent of the indicators have data on African countries (Statistics Division, 2017b).

Updates to data availability on the Sustainable Development Goals in Africa will be found in the ECA database, called ECAStats, following the revamping of the ECA statistical database maintained by the African Centre for Statistics. ECAStats has been set up as one of the portals containing Goal indicators on Africa, with accompanying metadata. At the Africa level, there are ongoing initiatives to develop a regional indicators framework that will be used to monitor progress on the 2030 Agenda and Agenda 2063. Because most of the regional indicators are taken from the global list of Goal indicators, it is essential that the ECA portal mirror African data available in the global Goal database of the Statistics Division, which is regularly updated as new data points become available.

iii Data quality

Data quality is another area of concern in Africa's statistical development. Efforts to improve data availability have not resulted in corresponding improvements in quality data production. Many African countries still face challenges in producing systematic, accurate, relevant, comparable and timely data. Key drivers of these shortcomings are differences in methodology, concepts and definitions used, a lack of coordination within the national statistics system, inadequate financial and human resources and weak infrastructure and data technology. These have contributed to significant discrepancies between data from various national sources and between national and regional and international sources. The Center for Global Development (2014) highlighted discrepancies between administrative data and household survey estimates in Africa with regard to education, agriculture, health and poverty. The use of various methodologies, concepts and definitions makes data comparability difficult.

iv Data accessibility and use

Data accessibility and use are a challenge in many countries owing to political issues, weak infrastructure and data technology, as well as inadequate capacity and funding. For example, data generated from censuses and surveys are often published late. There are efforts to use technology, including mobile devices and geospatial information, in censuses and surveys in a number of countries, which is helping to fill these gaps. The use of various formats by various data producers also limits data accessibility. Combined with the non-integration of user needs in data dissemination and publication policy, inadequate information on available data and how to access them create further uncertainties about the usability of data and actual usage (Kiregyera, 2015).

v Use of geospatial data

As the geospatial community works through the Sustainable Development Goals and their indicators, it is realizing that, among the existing data sets, there are a number of data gaps. Some of them are significant, not so much in their spatial resolution but in their temporal resolution. For example, a few of the indicators require more current data, while the data currently available to measure these indicators is three-to-four years out of date. Data production therefore needs to be more agile and adaptable to user requirements. This is a challenge for the professional community and requires partnerships with other organizations and the private sector, who often have a greater ability to generate data faster.

The United Nations Initiative on Global Geospatial Information Management is working closely with the statistical community at the national, regional and global levels to develop the global indicator framework with the inter-agency and expert group on the Sustainable Development Goal indicators. Bearing in mind that the accessibility of fundamental geospatial data is a prerequisite for calculating the indicators, there is need to build consensus on the need to integrate national spatial data infrastructure into national development plans. A strategy on such infrastructure that is aligned with sustainable development as an all-encompassing theme will provide the essential data and information for monitoring the indicators. It will also bring the analysis and evidence-base to the process and, therefore, a consistent monitoring and reporting framework to benefit all areas of government.

The Addis Ababa Action Agenda of the Third International Conference on Financing for Development provided a comprehensive framework for the international community to finance sustainable development. Financing the Sustainable Development Goals will require at least $1.5 trillion annually over what was required for the Millennium Development Goals ($120 billion annually). With respect to satellite-based Earth observation imagery, one estimate puts the investment required at $150 million for start-up costs and $5 million in annual costs covering all 77 countries receiving support from the International Development Association (IDA)[1] of the World Bank. (Digital Globe, 2015).

---

1 IDA is a multi-issue institution that provides loans and grants for development activities to poor countries at highly concessional rates. Eligibility for IDA support depends first and foremost on a country's relative poverty, defined as gross national income per capita below an established threshold ($1,215 in 2016). IDA also supports some countries, including small island economies that are above the per capita income threshold, but lack the creditworthiness required to borrow at non-concessional rates.

1.4 Statistics for progress reporting on the 2030 Agenda and Agenda 2063

1.4.1 Indicators for the 2030 Agenda and Agenda 2063: Africa's contribution

African countries are required to report progress on the implementation of 2030 Agenda and Agenda 2063, which requires large amounts of data. The 2030 Agenda has 17 Goals and 169 targets. In 2015, the Statistical Commission established the inter-agency and expert group on Sustainable Development Goal indicators to develop the monitoring and reporting framework for the 2030 Agenda. In March 2016, the Commission agreed on a set of 230 global indicators, subject to future technical refinement. The global list of indicators will be complemented by indicators at the continental and national levels. At the global level, the follow-up and review at the high-level political forum will be informed by the annual progress report on the Goals to be prepared by the Secretary-General in cooperation with the United Nations system, on the basis of the global indicator framework and data produced by national statistical systems and information collected at the regional level.

Agenda 2063 has 20 goals and 174 targets. Its results framework represents a logical relationship between the African Union vision, the seven African aspirations, the goal/priority areas under each aspiration and the associated targets. Following the adoption of Agenda 2063 by the heads of State and Governments of the African Union in January 2015, the African Union Commission prepared the first 10-year implementation plan, for the period 2014-2023. It contains 63 core indi-

> **Many African countries are in the process of aligning the global and continental development goals with their national development priorities, which entails efforts to harmonize, coordinate or integrate data requirements.**

cators for monitoring and reporting on Agenda 2063, of which 40 are identical to the Sustainable Development Goal indicators.

In 2016, the Conference of African Ministers of Finance, Planning and Economic Development encouraged pan-African institutions to adopt a coherent strategy for the effective and coordinated implementation of Agenda 2063 and the 2030 Agenda. The ministers agreed to a single monitoring and evaluation framework, accommodating both Agendas, and a common reporting architecture that will produce a single periodic performance report. They also acknowledged that the implementation of, reporting on and follow-up to both Agendas require a coherent strategy and an integrated set of goals, targets and indicators, along with a harmonized review and reporting platform.

Many African countries are in the process of aligning the global and continental development goals with their national development priorities, which entails efforts to harmonize, coordinate or integrate data requirements. The pan-African institutions are currently working on an integrated monitoring and evaluation framework that will be used to monitor and report on Agenda 2063 and the 2030 Agenda at the continent level. This requires large amounts of data to be produced and disseminated by countries.

1.4.2 Data availability and opportunities for reporting on Agenda 2063 and the 2030 Agenda

The Statistics Division led the development of the global Sustainable Development Goal database dissemination platform, which currently has a reasonable amount of data on the indicators (Statistics Division, 2017b). Of the 230 indicators, the portal has 91 on African countries, or 37.8 per cent of the total. TABLE 1.1 provides a summary of the sources of the data points in the database. Some of the indicators are disaggregated by sex, age group and location. There are also data for 33 additional indicators, which could help to measure the targets. In addition to data at the country level, aggregates are provided for Africa (excluding North Africa) and Northern Africa. The data are for the years 1990-

TABLE I.I   SUSTAINABLE DEVELOPMENT GOAL DATA AVAILABILITY ON AFRICAN COUNTRIES

SUSTAINABLE DEVELOPMENT GOAL	DATA AVAILABILITY BY INDICATOR TYPE			TOTAL NUMBER OF INDICATORS *	PERCENTAGE OF INDICATORS WITH DATA
	SUSTAINABLE DEVELOPMENT	ADDITIONAL	TOTAL		
1	3	3	6	12	25.0
2	8	4	12	14	57.1
3	18	7	25	26	69.2
4	6	3	9	11	54.5
5	3	1	5	14	21.4
6	2	4	6	11	18.2
7	4	0	4	6	66.7
8	10	1	11	17	58.8
9	8	1	9	12	66.7
10	5	0	5	11	45.5
11	1	1	2	15	6.7
12	2	1	3	14	14.3
13	0	0	0	9	0.0
14	1	0	1	7	14.3
15	6	0	6	14	42.9
16	6	5	11	23	26.1
17	8	3	11	25	32.0
Total	**91**	**33**	**124**	**241**	**37.8**

A total of 11 indicators are repeated.

2016. Globally, there are 139 indicators that require data in order to monitor and report on the relevant Goals and targets.

Some of the Sustainable Development Goals have data for more than half the indicators, such as Goal 3 (69.2 per cent), Goal 7 (66.7 per cent), Goal 9 (66.7 per cent), Goal 8 (58.8 per cent), Goal 2 (57.1 per cent) and Goal 4 (54.5 per cent). On the other hand, there are no data for all the indicators under Goal 13.

TABLE I.I highlights the need for strong efforts by African countries to align national development plans with the Sustainable Development Goals (Economic Commission for Africa et al., 2016). Efforts to this effect have begun in Côte d'Ivoire, Kenya, Nigeria, Senegal, South Africa and the United Republic of Tanzania

(Economic Commission for Africa, 2016). Building on investments in data production to monitor progress towards the Millennium Development Goals, a number of national statistical systems have some capacity to produce data to measure progress, especially in the social and economic dimensions of the Goals (i.e., Goals 1-4 and 6-10). With the exception of South Africa, which has the strongest national statistical capacity on the continent. Data production, dissemination and use with respect to Goals 11-15 remain relatively weak in many countries. In the United Republic of Tanzania, for example, most of the indicators in these areas are new to the national statistical system. A total of 27 indicators in these areas require new data collection systems, with 11 of them needing new systems with respect to Goal 15 alone.

1.4.3 Africa's contributions to informing the global database of Sustainable Development Goal indicators on Africa

The extent of indicators without data on Africa in the Global SDG database demonstrates the persistence of a data gap in national statistical systems (Statistics Division, 2017a). The sources of the data points in the global Sustainable Development Goal database are summarized in TABLE I.2. It can be observed that estimation, global monitoring and modelled data provide some 54 per cent of the total data on the Goals regarding Africa. Although there have been improvements in the share of country and country-adjusted data, from 22.8 per cent during the period 1990-2005 to 33.5 per cent during the period 2006-2016, the overall share for the whole duration was only 28.9 per cent.

During the period 2006-2016, the range of the country or country-adjusted data source lies between 16.6 per cent in Libya to 37.2 per cent in Mauritius. Countries with the share of country or country-adjusted data source below 20 per cent include Libya, Somalia (18.6 per cent) and South Sudan (18.8 per cent). On the other hand, more than one-third of data from South Africa (33.3 per cent), Ethiopia (33.7), Egypt (33.7 per cent), Cabo Verde (34.3 per cent), Niger (34.6 per cent), Ghana (35.9 per cent), Morocco (36.2 per cent) and Mauritius are country or country-adjusted. A total of 39 per cent of the indicators on Africa are estimated by international organizations.

This small share of data obtained from country sources stresses the need for further investment in the national statistical systems in order to develop capacity in a range of areas, such as administrative records and civil registration and vital statistics. This will help to improve the collection, analysis, dissemination and availability of accurate, timely and comparable data. Investment in data is also needed to support effective decision-making and monitoring of progress on national development plans and the dissemination of data among subregional, regional and international organizations that monitor and report on Agenda 2063 and the 2030 Agenda. Moreover, national statistical authorities need to work with other stakeholders, such as the private sector and civil society organizations that are involved in data-production activities.

1.4.4 Advocacy for action

The Sustainable Development Goals require that all the actors, stakeholders and beneficiaries have access to relevant information to play their relevant roles in the development process, including implementing, monitoring and reporting on progress. The relevant information should always include official statistics.

Notwithstanding notable progress made by African countries in the production and dissemination of statistics during the past decade or so, official statistics produced by national statistical systems are not always available in forms that allow easy access. Therefore, monitoring the broad range of development issues

TABLE I.2   DATA SOURCES OF SUSTAINABLE DEVELOPMENT GOAL INDICATORS ON AFRICA

DATA SOURCE TYPE	1990 - 2005		2006 - 2016		1990 - 2016	
	TOTAL DATA POINTS	SHARE (%)	TOTAL DATA POINTS	SHARE (%)	TOTAL DATA POINTS	SHARE (%)
Country or country-adjusted	7 948	22.8	15 443	33.5	23 391	28.9
Estimation	14 981	42.9	16 600	36.0	31 581	39.0
Global monitoring	2 672	7.7	4 867	10.6	7 539	9.3
Modelling	1 957	5.6	2 656	5.8	4 613	5.7
Others	7 336	21.0	6 493	14.1	13 829	17.1
Total	**34 894**	**100**	**46 059**	**100**	**80 953**	**100**

Source: Global Sustainable Development Goal database. Available from www.un.org/en/africa/osaa/peace/agenda2063.shtml.

covered by the Sustainable Development Goals and the need to fulfil the principle of disaggregation along dimensions of, among others, age, gender, income and geography constitute an additional challenge to the already weak statistical systems that lack adequate technological infrastructure and to financial and human resource capacities.

The measurement of progress towards achieving the Sustainable Development Goals and those contained Agenda 2063 necessitates investing massively in statistics to fill the gaps that limit the generation of quality, relevant, timely and comparable data, including capacity gaps and technology (Economic Commission for Africa, 2016). Investing in statistics can provide excellent returns. It stands not only to benefit evidence-based decision-making and monitoring, but also to strengthen the overall statistical system by building capacity in a range of areas, such as the accuracy of administrative records and improved data analysis and dissemination.

The cost of these investments, however, in particular data collection for the 2030 Agenda, Agenda 2063 and national development priorities, will be very high if it is to be met by the official statistics community alone. Collaboration among various data communities and the coordination, harmonization and integration of data from various sources within data ecosystems will therefore be helpful in filling in gaps in official statistics, reducing costs and enhancing data accessibility and use (Economic Commission for Africa, 2016). There are capacities and resources to be tapped within the national data ecosystems, such as the private sector, civil society, academia, citizenry and open data communities.

The Sustainable Development Goals require that all the actors, stakeholders and beneficiaries have access to relevant information to play their relevant roles in the development process, including implementing, monitoring and reporting on progress.

The measurement of progress towards achieving the Sustainable Development Goals and those contained Agenda 2063 necessitates investing massively in statistics to fill the gaps that limit the generation of quality, relevant, timely and comparable data, including capacity gaps and technology.

The need for collaboration among various data communities was also a key element of discussions concerning statistical capacity for the post-2015 development agenda that called for a wider range of actors to be involved in the development of statistical methods, such as data scientists and geospatial specialists from the private sector and research community, government officials and other data users. These requirements were echoed by the high-level panel of eminent persons that went further and called for a "data revolution"[2] for development.

The data revolution can be harnessed to catalyse positive social, economic and environmental transformation in Africa. The increasing demand for data and statistics under the 2030 Agenda and Agenda 2063 is an opportunity for Africa to embark on the data revolution in order to improve statistical capacity in all domains, given that their adoption coincides with unprecedented innovation in data technologies used to collect data and analyse and disseminate a huge volume and type of data, leading to the availability and use of bigger and more detailed data than before (Independent Expert Advisory Group on the Data Revolution for Sustainable Development, 2014). Considerable innovation and experimentation is currently under way within multiple data communities and ecosystems in African countries. For the most part, however, these are small-scale and

2   The term "data revolution" refers to a "rapid increase in the volume of data, speed of data production, number of data producers, dissemination of data, and the range of things on which there is data, supported by new technologies e.g. mobile phones and the 'internet of things', and from other sources, such as qualitative data, citizen-generated data and perceptions data; and growing demand for data from all parts of society" (Independent Expert Advisory Group on the Data Revolution for Sustainable Development, 2014).

often isolated initiatives. If Africa is to benefit from the full transformative potential of the data revolution, more systematic, large-scale, integrated and sustainable efforts are going to be needed (Economic Commission for Africa, 2015).

African Governments recognize the importance of the data revolution as embodied in the Africa data consensus (Economic Commission for Africa et al., 2015) and other statistical and development initiatives, including the African Charter on Statistics and the African Union's strategy for the harmonization of statistics in Africa. The consensus is a strategy for implementing the data revolution in Africa that was adopted at a high-level conference on the data revolution, held in March 2015, in response to calls for a framework on the data revolution in Africa and its implications for Agenda 2063 and the 2030 Agenda.

At the national level, this can be seen in long-term national development plans, and numerous changes, reforms and innovations are needed to enable member States to embark on a data revolution. In this regard, access to and the use of new sources of data, in particular big data, to complement official statistics is needed. This requires strategic and innovative partnerships and collaboration between national statistical systems and other actors of various data communities. A challenge in this collaboration is that big data do not always follow statistical principles, making it difficult for the analysis and generation of results. In this respect, a lot of work in terms of, among other things, methodologies, definitions and classifications is required. Moreover, some issues, such as technical, legal, proprietary and privacy issues relating to big data, limit their effective access and use, notwithstanding their timeliness and cost-effectiveness (Robin et al., 2016). Legal, legislative and policy reforms are required to address these issues. According to the guidelines of the national strategy for the development of statistics on the data revolution, "by providing a legal framework for countries to guide their own legislative processes, the Charter indeed provides leverage and guidelines that help in modifying the law accounting for new data developments, such as the use of Big Data".[3]

The adoption of open data principles for both national statistical systems and other national data ecosystems is one of the most effective approaches to making data available to a wide audience. Open data are online, free of cost and accessible, and can be used, reused and redistributed, subject only, at most, to the requirements to attribute and to share.

> The data revolution can be harnessed to catalyse positive social, economic and environmental transformation in Africa. The increasing demand for data and statistics under the 2030 Agenda and Agenda 2063 is an opportunity for Africa to embark on the data revolution.

The improvement in existing data sources is also key to effective progress monitoring. Census survey and administrative data are the main sources of data used to inform the 2030 Agenda and Agenda 2063. This requires improvement in the coverage and frequency of censuses and surveys, and the modernization of administrative systems, including civil registration and vital statistics. It entails significant investment in data technologies, capacity, infrastructure and human and financial resources.

The development of the national spatial data infrastructure is needed for capacity-building, funding, coordination, fundamental data sets and reference systems. Capacity needs and data gap assessments will help to support efforts towards statistical development within the framework of the 2030 Agenda and Agenda 2063 at the national, regional and international levels.

---

3   Available from www.paris21.org/nsdsguidelines.

1.5 Conclusion

Previous efforts to monitor and report progress of the Millennium Development Goals and other initiatives led to increased government and development partner investments to improve national statistical systems and data availability. Further work is needed to strengthen the capacities of member States in the production, analysis, storage, dissemination and use of statistical data. Additional funding, embracing new data sources and innovations and geospatial information are required. Initiatives on statistical development have to take into account challenges discussed above so that African countries can produce and disseminate adequate, high-quality and timely statistical data for monitoring the implementation of their national development plans and to report on the progress in achieving the Sustainable Development Goals and the goals contained in Agenda 2063.

In the Africa data consensus, the following key actions are underscored to support the data revolution for effective monitoring of the 2030 Agenda and Agenda 2063 in African countries:

- Create an inclusive data ecosystem involving Government, the private sector, academia, civil society, local communities and development partners that tackles the informational aspects of development decision-making in a coordinated way. Governments must play a proactive role in engaging this community, and other stakeholders should prioritize partnership with Government. This is linked to the strategy for statistical development. Existing national strategies for the development of statistics should be revised to make them more inclusive of all data communities

Further work is needed to strengthen the capacities of member States in the production, analysis, storage, dissemination and use of statistical data.

- As a critical first step towards strengthening the data ecosystem, review the capacity needs, legal and financial frameworks, participating institutions, data assets and gaps at the national, subnational and community levels to recognize the roles of the various stakeholders and create a workable road map with clear milestones

- Have Governments take the lead in ensuring that the recurrent costs of production and dissemination of all required data is financed from sustainable national resources. A resource mobilization strategy should be put in place

- Have Governments identify a body authorized to provide credentials to data communities providing open data on the basis of established criteria for quality, reliability, timeliness and relevance to statistical information needs

- Develop civil registration systems that produce credible vital statistics that are a cornerstone of the data revolution. Likewise, population, economic, labour, health, education, land and agricultural management information systems should be supported to ensure timely and accurate data to drive decision-making at the national and subnational levels

- Adopt, foster and strengthen public-private partnerships as a strategy for knowledge and technology transfer and to promote sustainable collaboration, funding and the sharing of experiences

- Extend, where applicable, all international norms and standards relating to official statistics to all data in order to improve their validity and credibility

- Promote innovative and integrated methodologies and technologies, including geospatial technology, to improve data collection, analysis and usage. It is important to integrate gender statistics and gender-specific indicators into monitoring and evaluation

- Have pan-African institutions, such as AfDB, the African Union Commission and ECA take the lead in the realization of the Africa data consensus, in partnership with other development partners.

CHAPTER 2

Sustainable Development Goal 1: End poverty in all its forms everywhere

2.1 Introduction

The objective of Sustainable Development Goal 1 is to end to poverty in all its manifestations, including extreme poverty, over the next 15 years beginning in 2016. All people everywhere, including the poorest and most vulnerable, should enjoy a basic standard of living and the benefits of adequate social protection. Indeed, eradicating poverty remains one of the greatest global challenges today, hence the continued focus on this overarching goal in the 2030 Agenda and in Agenda 2063.

... eradicating poverty remains one of the greatest global challenges today, hence the continued focus on this overarching goal in the 2030 Agenda and in Agenda 2063.

2.2 Targets and alignment with Agenda 2063

Sustainable Development Goal 1 has 7 targets and 12 indicators and is aligned with goal 1 of Agenda 2063, which has 12 related targets (see TABLE 2.1). Data on this Goal are, in general, available at the international level for at least three of the seven targets. Data availability at the country level presents a mixed picture, with considerable gaps in quality, timeliness and the level of disaggregation. For the purposes of this report, reference is made mostly to the Goal indicators and targets, while not losing sight of the continental agenda.

2.3 Progress in poverty reduction

... the non-inclusiveness of growth, inequalities, food insecurity, population dynamics and fragility to shocks continue to challenge Africa's poverty reduction agenda.

As a more expansive and ambitious development agenda, the 2030 Agenda builds on the legacy of the Millennium Development Goals framework, which ended in December 2015. Significant progress was made on most of the social development ills that faced the world at the turn of the century. By 2012, approximately one in every eight people around the world lived in extreme poverty (United Nations, 2016a; see BOX 2.1). The global picture, however, masks challenges in meeting the target of reducing poverty by 2030 in other regions of the world, such as Africa (excluding North Africa) and Oceania, where income poverty has remained widespread, notwithstanding efforts to

SDG 1 TARGETS	ALIGNMENT TO AGENDA 2063: GOALS 1, 5, 7, 17, 20* TARGETS
1.1 By 2030, eradicate extreme poverty for all people everywhere, currently measured as people living on less than $1.25 a day	**1.1.2.1** Reduce 2013 levels of poverty by at least 30%.
1.2 By 2030, reduce at least by half the proportion of men, women and children of all ages living in poverty in all its dimensions according to national definitions	**1.1.2.1** Reduce 2013 levels of poverty by at least 30%. **1.1.2.2** Reduce poverty amongst women by at least 50%
1.3 Implement nationally appropriate social protection systems and measures for all, including floors, and by 2030 achieve substantial coverage of the poor and the vulnerable	**1.1.3.1** At least 30% of vulnerable populations including persons with disabilities, older persons and children provided with social protection.
1.4 By 2030, ensure that all men and women, in particular the poor and the vulnerable, have equal rights to economic resources, as well as access to basic services, ownership and control over land and other forms of property, inheritance, natural resources, appropriate new technology and financial services, including microfinance	**1.1.4.10** At least 70% of the population indicate an increase in access to quality basic services (water, sanitation, electricity, transportation, internet connectivity **6.17.1.1** Equal economic rights for women, including the rights to own and inherit property, sign a contract, save, register and manage a business and own and operate a bank account by 2026 **6.17.1.2.** At least 20% of women in rural areas have access to and control productive assets, including land and grants, credit, inputs, financial service and information
1.5 By 2030, build the resilience of the poor and those in vulnerable situations and reduce their exposure and vulnerability to climate-related extreme events and other economic, social and environmental shocks and disasters	**1.7.3.3** Reduce deaths and property loss from natural and man-made disasters and climate extreme events by at least 30% **1.5.1.5** Increase the proportion of farm, pastoral and fisher households are resilient to climate and weather related risks to 30%
1.a Ensure significant mobilization of resources from a variety of sources, including through enhanced development cooperation, in order to provide adequate and predictable means for developing countries, in particular least developed countries, to implement programmes and policies to end poverty in all its dimensions	**1.1.2.1** Reduce 2013 levels of poverty by at least 30%.
1.b Create sound policy frameworks at the national, regional and international levels, based on pro-poor and gender-sensitive development strategies, to support accelerated investment in poverty eradication actions	**1.1.2.2** Reduce poverty amongst women by at least 50%

Source: Authors' own analysis based on Statistics Division (2017b) and African Union Commission (2015).

" Goal 1 (a high standard of living, quality of life and well-being for all), goal 5 (modern agriculture for increased productivity and production) and goal 7 (environmentally sustainable climate-resilient economies and communities) of aspiration 1; goal 17 (full gender equality in all spheres of life) of aspiration 6; and goal 20 (Africa takes full responsibility for financing her development) of aspiration 7.

BOX 2.1 GLOBAL POVERTY: OVERVIEW

At least 13 per cent of the global population lived in extreme poverty in 2012, down from 26 per cent in 2000. One in eight people worldwide lived in extreme poverty in 2012; in 2015, at least 10 per cent of the world's workers and their families lived on less than $1.90 per person per day, down from 28 per cent in 2000. Young people between 15 and 24 years of age are more likely to be among the working poor: 16 per cent of employed young people were living in poverty in 2015, compared with 9 per cent of working adults. A total of 20 per cent of people received social assistance or social protection benefits in low-income countries, compared with 67 per cent in upper-middle-income countries.

Source: United Nations, (2016a).

reduce poverty substantially between 2000 and 2015. By 2013, poverty rates, using the income measure of $1.90/day, in Africa (excluding North Africa) had been reduced by at least 15 per cent, from the 1990 rate of 56.9 per cent to 41 per cent (World Bank, 2016b), with the fastest reductions occurring between 2002 and 2012. Strong growth and concerted efforts towards human development improvements through the Millennium Development Goal agenda accounted for most of that progress, although the non-inclusiveness of growth, inequalities, food insecurity, population dynamics and fragility to shocks continue to challenge Africa's poverty reduction agenda.

Strong economic performance, coupled with increases in official development assistance (ODA) between the mid-2000s and 2013, provided the fiscal space for most countries to increase expenditure in education, health and agriculture. Unfortunately, the onset of the economic downturn in 2014, triggered by many factors, including the Ebola epidemic, widespread droughts, floods and the decline in commodity prices, has had significant negative effects on Africa's social economic development (see FIGURE 2.1) on the general trends in economic growth since 2010.

FIGURE 2.1   SUBREGIONAL TRENDS IN GDP GROWTH AND ANNUAL GDP GROWTH BY REGION, 2010–2015

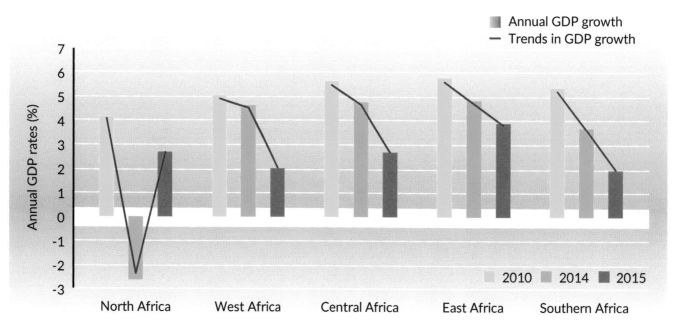

Source: 2016 World Bank world development indicators data.

In 2015, economic growth on the continent was somewhat subdued, with drops in all regions, except for a notable rebound in North Africa (see FIGURE 2.1), buoyed by strong performances in a few countries within those subregions. In North Africa, for example, strong growth in Algeria, Egypt and Morocco pushed the regional average up significantly, while sharp downturns in Sierra Leone, Liberia, Guinea and Nigeria had an overall negative effect on West Africa's growth prospects, despite strong growth in Cote d'ivoire, Guinea Bissau, Mali, Senegal and Togo.

On the other hand, the overall performance in Central, East and Southern Africa, was affected by large economic contractions in a number of countries, primarily those that depend on oil or minerals. Such contractions were seen in Botswana, Chad, Equatorial Guinea, South Africa, South Sudan, Zambia and Zimbabwe, while Ethiopia, Kenya, Mozambique, Rwanda, Uganda and the United Republic of Tanzania continued to shore up East Africa's steady growth, with an average annual growth rate of 6.76 per cent (see FIGURE 2.2).

Such volatility, although normal in cycles of growth, is not conducive to sustained efforts towards poverty reduction, especially for economies that do not have the means to cushion themselves against shocks in order to avoid development reversals that are often seen on the continent. Poverty eradication, or a 30 per cent reduction, in accordance with the Agenda 2063 target, will depend in large part on the reinforcing interactions between Sustainable Development Goal 8 for inclusive growth of at least 7 per cent annually in order to provide decent jobs for all, including women and young people; the provision of education, health care and other social services for improved human development (Goals 3, 4, 6 and 15); a reduction in inequalities through Goals 5 and 10, including the provision of social safety nets; and sustainable land use that would enhance food security, promote diversification and combat climate change (Goals 12-14).

The 2030 Agenda and Agenda 2063 have the potential to lay the foundation for sustainable development in which poverty and inequalities can be reduced significantly, if implemented properly. For the Africa region, it will be imperative to monitor progress made on these interrelated goals over time in order to track achievements of the overarching goal of poverty reduction, namely, goal 1 under aspiration 1 of Agenda 2063, towards a high standard of living, quality of life and well-being for all, which is supportive of global development priorities.

Both Sustainable Development Goal 1 and goal 1 of Agenda 2063 call for an end to poverty in all its dimensions and include targets to ensure that measures are taken to support the most vulnerable population groups through the provision of social safety nets and the reduction in inequalities in employment among men, women and young people. The following sections will therefore show the poverty trends in Africa against the targets set in Goal 1 and, wherever possible, goal 1 of Agenda 2063, which will be used as benchmarks for monitoring and analysing future progress on this Goal. The next section assesses progress made on each of the targets with sufficient data.

Target 1.1 of Sustainable Development Goal 1

> By 2030, eradicate extreme poverty for all people everywhere, currently measured as people living on less than $1.25 a day

Related Agenda 2063 target:

i   Reduce 2013 levels of poverty by at least 30 per cent.

Substantial progress has been made towards reducing poverty on the continent, although challenges remain, in particular outside North Africa. North Africa has made the most progress in reducing poverty globally: between 1990 and 2012, poverty rates declined by some 70 per cent. Africa (excluding North Africa), on the other hand, continues to face significant challenges in this regard and has the highest poverty rates in the world, with rates of more than 40 per cent in 2012 and 2013,[1] second only to Oceania (see FIGURE 2.3). Nevertheless, poverty rates are down by at least 15 per cent from the 1990 figures, demonstrating progress in the right direction.

The pace of poverty reduction in Africa (excluding North Africa) has been slower than anticipated due to the region's structural challenges and its lack of resilience to shocks, which makes it susceptible to many reversals. The reductions to date appear to have been

---

1   Using the latest World Bank data, the poverty rate for Africa (excluding North Africa) was 41 per cent in 2013. The World Bank data combine North Africa with the Middle East, which makes comparison between Africa (excluding North Africa) and North Africa alone challenging. The trends on poverty between data from Statistics Division and the World Bank are largely the same. Both sources of data have been used in this report without affecting the analysis of each set.

FIGURE 2.2 GDP GROWTH RATES, 2005-2014

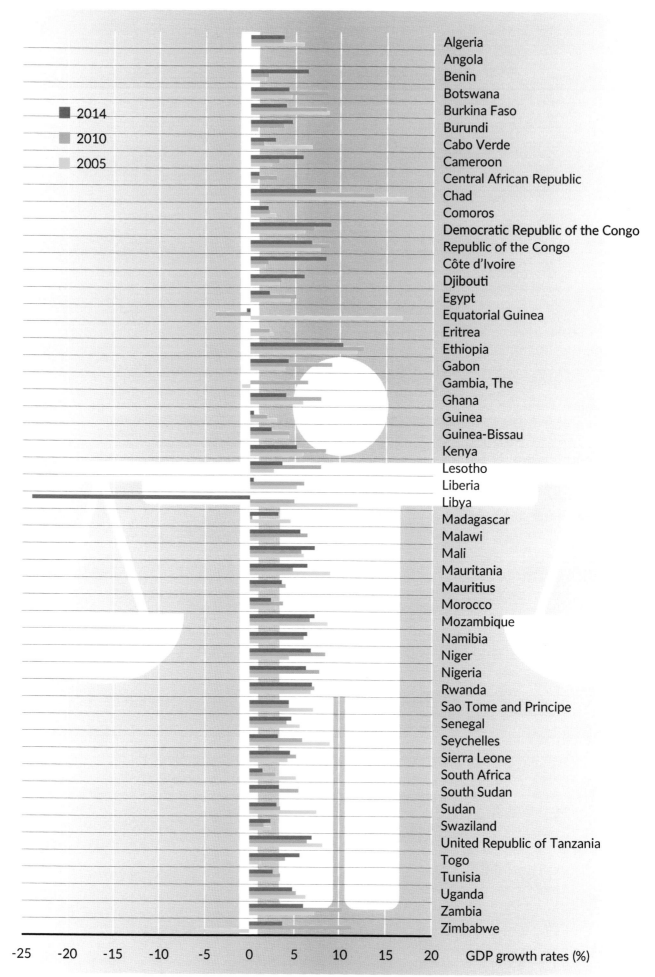

Source: 2016 World Bank world development indicators data.

FIGURE 2.3 PROPORTION OF PEOPLE LIVING BELOW $1.90/DAY, 2002-2013

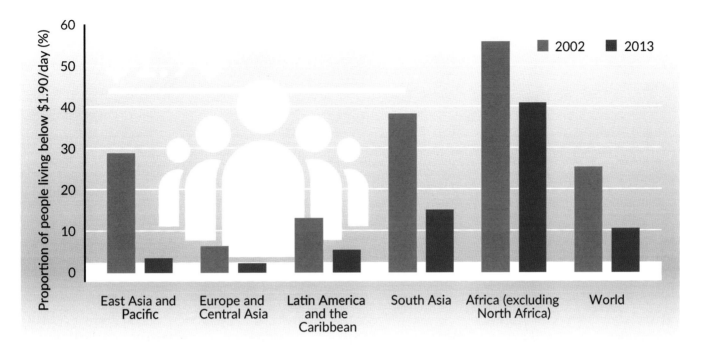

Source: World Bank (2016).

attained on the back of relatively strong growth, averaging 5 per cent annually since the mid-2000s, and concerted efforts through the Millennium Development Goals framework. Even with such efforts, the region managed to reduce poverty only by an average of 1.5 per cent annually between 2002 and 2012, compared with a 2.7 per cent reduction annually on average for all developing regions combined (see FIGURE 2.4). Further reductions would require substantial investment in growth that is inclusive in order to have an impact on income poverty and on other investment that would address other dimensions of poverty. The pace of poverty reduction per region in presented in FIGURE 2.4.

FIGURE 2.4 CHANGES IN POVERTY RATES, 2002-2012

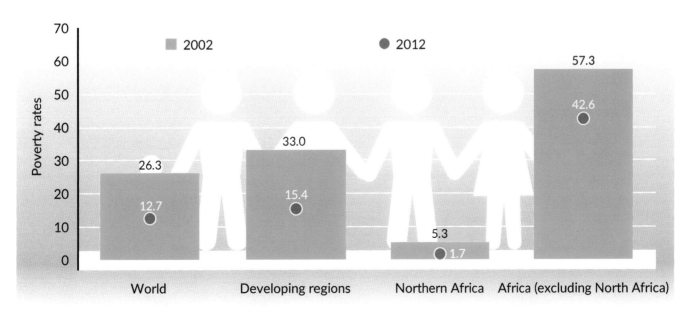

Source: Statistics Division (2016).

Target 1.2 of Sustainable Development Goal 1

By 2030, reduce at least by half the proportion of men, women and children of all ages living in poverty in all its dimension according to national definitions

Related Agenda 2063 targets:

i   Reduce 2013 levels of poverty by at least 30 per cent;

ii Reduce poverty among women by at least 50 per cent.

Africa has the largest share of working poor in the world, notwithstanding declining trends. Since 2000, the proportion of working populations living in extreme poverty has been declining, with notable regional differences. Initial conditions still play a big role in the rest of Africa, which had the highest proportion of working poor at the beginning of the implementation of the Millennium Development Goals, highlighting the importance of structural transformation and decent jobs. Over 52.8 per cent of the working population in the rest of Africa lived under $1.90 a day, compared with 8.1 per cent in North Africa in 2000 (see FIGURE 2.5).

By 2015, Africa (excluding North Africa) had one third of its working population living in extreme poverty, compared with more than half its working population in 2000. South Asia is the only other region that had initial conditions comparable to the rest of Africa. Economies in that region, however, have managed to create decent jobs and substantially reduce the poverty levels of its working population in general. Between 2000 and 2015, South Asia reduced its poverty rates among the working poor by at least 24 per cent. Economic and technological advancements have fuelled most of the progress in that region, which has assisted in the creation of decent jobs for most people.

Africa's working poor are often engaged in vulnerable employment, with low returns on their labour, rendering this population group most at risk of falling back into poverty even when advances are made for the better. The share of people in vulnerable employment remains unacceptably high, at almost 60 per cent in 2014 (see FIGURE 2.6), often heavily skewed towards young people and women, which will continue to challenge the achievement of the Sustainable Development Goals and the aspiration contained in Agenda 2063 to reduce poverty by 30 per cent by 2023.

FIGURE 2.5   PROPORTION OF WORKING POPULATION LIVING UNDER $1.90 PER DAY

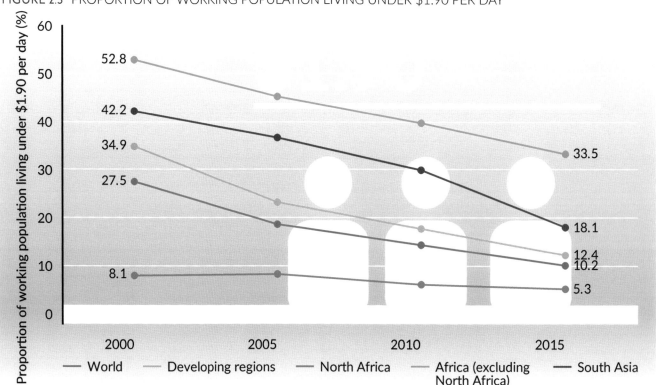

Source: Statistics Division (2016).

FIGURE 2.6 VULNERABLE EMPLOYMENT PER REGION

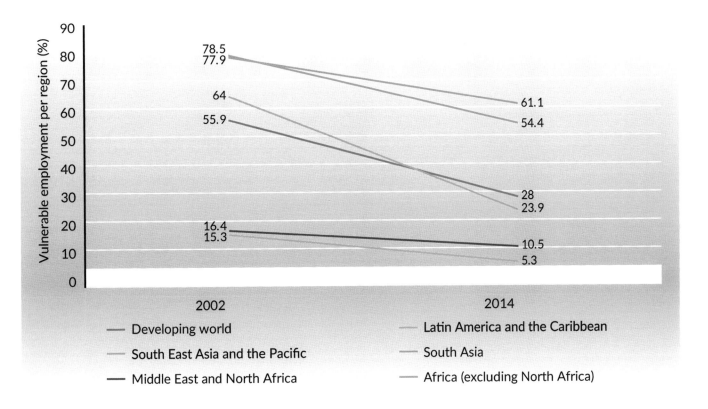

Source: International Labour Organization statistics (2016).

With regard to the proportion of employed people living in poverty by age and sex, working young people and women continue to be disproportionately affected by the burden of poverty. In all regions, the burden of poverty is much higher among young people and women, notwithstanding declining trends over time. Inequalities by age are particularly large in developing regions as a whole, but much higher in the rest of Africa, Oceania and South Asia, where initial conditions were much higher than the rest of the world in 2000. On the continent, following the general poverty trends, the gap between adults and young people has been especially wide when comparing North Africa with the rest of Africa. The poverty levels of young working people have been consistently higher than the adult working population in all regions. They are more likely to be poor than adults and more likely to migrate, show discontent or seek alternative means of survival, which may threaten development progress. On the other hand, this is a population group that holds much promise for higher development pathways that needs to be harnessed for that dividend to be realized.

Although the general trend is the same in all regions, regional variations exist in response to subregional political and economic dynamics. For example, the gap between the adult working poor and young people fell

The share of people in vulnerable employment remains unacceptably high, at almost 60 per cent in 2014, often heavily skewed towards young people and women.

FIGURE 2.7 PROPORTION OF WORKERS LIVING BELOW THE POVERTY LINE BY AGE

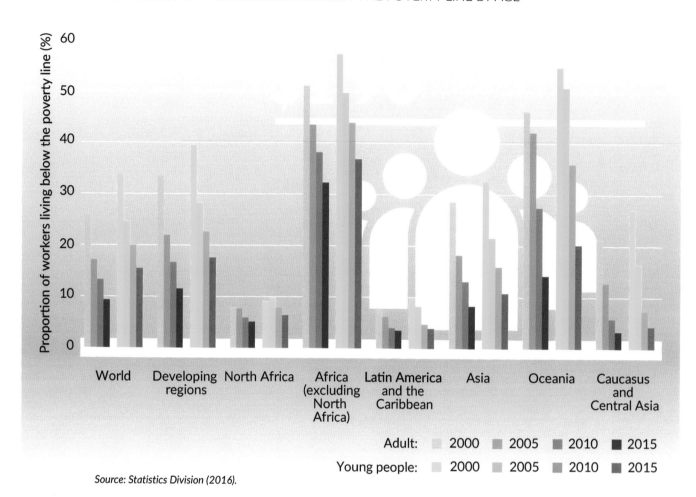

Source: Statistics Division (2016).

marginally over the years, from 6.2 per cent in 2000 to 5.8 per cent in 2010 and 4.6 per cent in 2015 (see FIGURE 2.7).

North Africa as a whole has experienced a slightly different picture. In 2000, the gap between adult and young people living in extreme poverty was only 1.3 per cent, but widened considerably to 2.0 per cent by 2010 before falling again to 1.3 per cent in 2015. Factors that contributed to that trend are common to the entire continent but were more pronounced in North Africa by 2010. The rising population of young people (which has the potential to be a demographic time bomb for the continent), rising unemployment, low living standards and rampant corruption, among other reasons, have been widening poverty gaps and engendering discontentment throughout the region. The Arab Spring, which began in Tunisia in 2011 as a response to popular discontentment within the country, in particular among young people, spread quickly throughout North Africa and the entire Arab region. Although the rest of Africa did not inevitably respond

in the same fashion as in the Arab Spring, it has had its fair share of demonstrations and flash points of fragility, which have crippled economic activity in countries such as South Africa, all stemming from feelings of disenfranchisement due to widespread poverty and a lack of jobs with decent wages.

Notwithstanding declining trends, working women continue to bear the brunt of poverty, as do young people. While poverty is, in general, declining among men and women in all regions, a higher proportion of working women still live in poverty compared to men. With the focused attention on gender equality through the Millennium Development Goal agenda, there has been notable progress to reduce the gender gap globally, although challenges remain. Reductions in the gender gap relating to poverty have been faster in Oceania, of all regions, where the proportions were comparable to Africa (excluding North Africa) in 2000, but had been reduced by at least 30 per cent and eliminated entirely by 2015 (see FIGURE 2.9).

FIGURE 2.8 GENDER DISTRIBUTION OF THE TOTAL WORKING POOR BY REGION

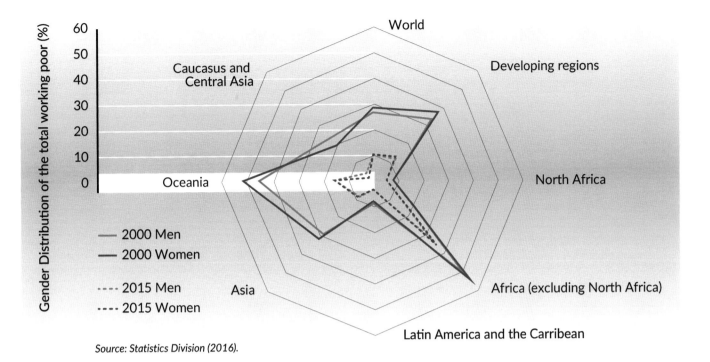

Source: Statistics Division (2016).

For Africa (excluding North Africa), where disparities remain large, there was a reduction in the proportion of working women living in poverty, from 54.8 per cent in 2000 (compared with 51.3 per cent of men) to 35.1 per cent in 2015 (compared with 32.1 per cent of men) (see FIGURE 2.9). Although this is encouraging, it is important to note that the actual gap between men and women, which stands at 3.5 per cent on average, had been reduced by only 0.5 basis points between 2000 and 2015. North Africa, on the other hand, managed to reduce the proportion of its working poor from its 2000 levels with a less linear pattern.

FIGURE 2.9 PROPORTION OF EMPLOYED POPULATION BELOW THE POVERTY LINE BY SEX

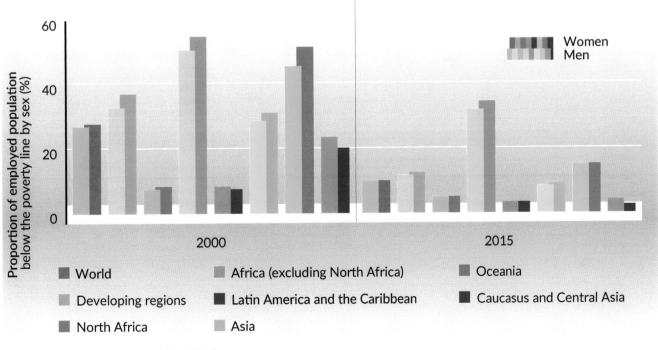

Source: Statistics Division (2016).

In 2000, the region had 8.2 per cent of its working women living in poverty, compared with 8 per cent of men, which was reduced to 5.4 per cent and 5.2 per cent in 2015, respectively. Overall, there has not been any change in reducing the actual gender gap between working men and women, which has stood at 0.2 per cent since 2000.

Although the gap is much narrower and the proportions much less than the global average, reaching these last pockets of deprivation will be a real challenge for most countries, not least, those in North Africa, if they are to leave no one behind in the implementation of the 2030 Agenda.

Target 1.3 of Sustainable Development Goal 1

Implement nationally appropriate social protection systems and measures for all, including floors, and by 2030 achieve substantial coverage of the poor and the vulnerable

Related Agenda 2063 targets:

i   At least 30 per cent of vulnerable populations, including children with disabilities, older persons and children, provided with social protection;

ii   All persons working in the formal sector are provided with social security;

... less than 1 per cent of the unemployed population receives any form of support.

iii   At least 20 per cent of the informal sector and rural labour have access to social security.

The proportion of the population covered by social protection systems is small, with low levels of social protection coverage holding back poverty reduction efforts in Africa. In combination with strong and inclusive growth, social assistance programmes and systems play an important role in significantly reducing poverty and inequalities around the world. Such recognition is what inspired the inclusion of social protection mechanisms as targets in the 2030 Agenda and Agenda 2063. Poverty levels are significantly lower in regions where there are combined efforts to increase economic productivity, with the provision of targeted social assistance such as unemployment benefits, social assistance, social insurance and other cash transfers. However, for Africa as a whole, less than 1 per cent of the unemployed population receives any form of support, let alone population groups engaged in vulnerable employment (see FIGURE 2.10). On the other hand, in developed regions, most unemployed people receive unemployment benefits. Poorer countries are unable

FIGURE 2.10 PROPORTION OF UNEMPLOYED RECEIVING UNEMPLOYMENT BENEFITS

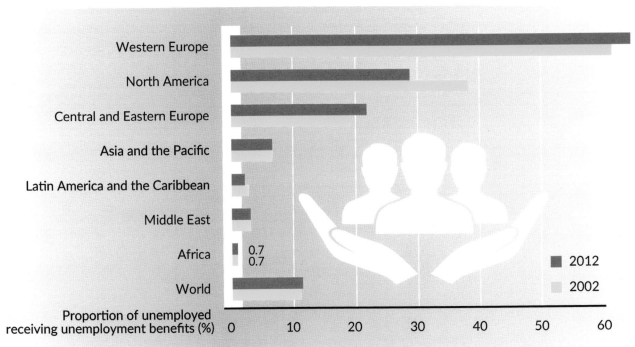

Source: Statistics Division (2016).

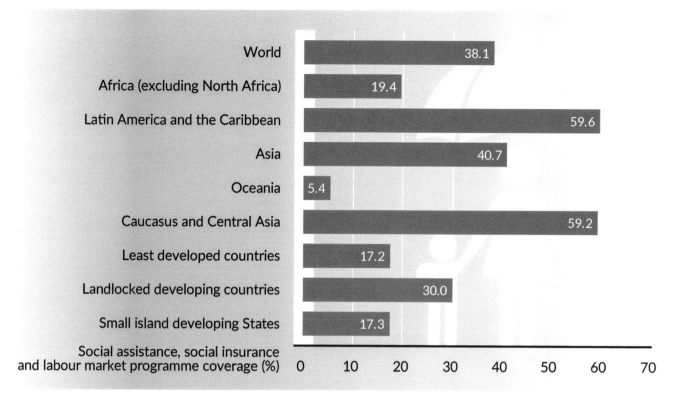

Source: Statistics Division (2016).

to provide comprehensive unemployment benefits to affected population groups, in part because of the magnitudes involved, low revenue collections and costs to the treasury.

While it difficult for developing regions to provide unemployment benefits, efforts are being made to provide other social assistance programmes to people living in extreme poverty. The impact has been positive in countries that have comprehensive programmes, such as those in Latin America (e.g., Brazil), in the Caucasus and Central Asia and in Asia, where the investment has been relatively high – at least more than 40 per cent. Africa (excluding North Africa) has been increasing its coverage over the years (an average of 19 per cent) (see FIGURE 2.II). The challenge has always been the sustenance of such programmes by most Governments and development actors in the face of economic downturns or cutbacks.

Poverty levels are significantly lower in regions where there are combined efforts to increase economic productivity, with the provision of targeted social assistance such as unemployment benefits, social assistance, social insurance and other cash transfers.

CHAPTER 2   SUSTAINABLE DEVELOPMENT GOAL I: END POVERTY IN ALL ITS FORMS EVERYWHERE

2.4 Conclusion

Poverty rates in Africa have been declining slowly. Large variations exist between North Africa and the rest of Africa, with the former having managed to reduce its poverty rates to under 2 per cent in 2012, while the latter still faces widespread poverty, with more than 40 per cent of its population living below the poverty line. Poverty eradication will increasingly require multiple and integrated strategies to address the many dimensions of poverty, such as ensuring sustained inclusive growth and addressing income poverty through decent jobs and labour market interventions and access to services that contribute to human development through multiple interventions in health, education, clean water, sanitation and other inequality-reducing measures, such as social safety nets and grants.

The regional picture masks individual country performances, however, in which outcomes are varied, with considerable gaps in evidence and data. Investments have to be made in strengthening data systems within countries to enable evidence-based planning, implementation and reporting. Reaching the last mile and leaving no one behind will require having available information on the poor, their gender, age group, geographical location and binding constraints.

In the face of widespread poverty, focused attention will have to be paid to the most vulnerable of populations groups. Unless data gaps are addressed, unfortunately, evidence-based policymaking will remain a challenge for most of Africa.

Poverty eradication will increasingly require multiple and integrated strategies to address the many dimensions of poverty.

CHAPTER 3

Sustainable Development Goal 2: Zero hunger

3.1 Introduction

Although progress has been made, hunger and food insecurity are still key development challenges for Africa. While some 194 million people on the continent are severely food insecure, another 161 million are moderately food insecure. Countries in the Sahel and Southern Africa were particularly hit by severe droughts arising from the El Niño phenomenon, which were aggravated by the culmination of several disruptive events, including internal conflicts. The livelihoods of affected communities have been severely disrupted and have required food assistance. These challenges have had a significant impact on the region's progress regarding acute malnutrition, undernourishment and food insecurity.

This chapter provides an assessment of the progress made in achieving Sustainable Development Goal 2, namely, to end hunger, achieve food security and improve nutrition and promote sustainable agriculture, and a comparison of its performance with the rest of the world. Since the Goals came in effect in 2016, countries are still making efforts to put systems in place for the implementation and monitoring of and reporting on them. Most countries have yet to prioritize targets and indicators and set the baselines, given that the data requirements are enormous. This chapter therefore provides an update on the status, as gauged by the relevant targets and indicators and trend analysis, where data are available.

> **Although progress has been made, hunger and food insecurity are still key development challenges for Africa.**

3.2 Targets and alignment with Agenda 2063

Sustainable Development Goal 2 has 8 targets and 14 indicators and is aligned with the following goals contained in Agenda 2063: goal 1 (a high standard of living, quality of life and well-being); goal 3 (healthy and well-nourished citizens); goal 4 (transformed economies and job creation); goal 5 (modern agriculture for increased productivity and production); goal 7 (environmentally sustainable climate-resilient economies and communities); and goal 8 (united Africa (federal or confederate)) (see TABLE 3.1).

This chapter provides information on the status of the progress made in reducing hunger and improving food security, as well as suggestions for the policy direction required to achieve the Sustainable Development Goals and the goals contained in Agenda 2063. The analysis highlights several key issues and challenges. First, Africa is making significant progress in several areas relating to hunger and food security, but remains fragile to shocks and is well below its potential for food production as reflected by the progress made in other regions of the world. The prevalence of undernourishment in North Africa remained low, at below 5 per cent, from 2000 to 2016, while it dropped from 30 to 22.9 per cent in Africa (excluding North Africa) during the same period. Across the whole of Africa, some 217 million people were undernourished in the period 2014-2016, an increase of 6 per cent from the 2010-2012 period. Meanwhile, the prevalence of severe food insecurity decreased, from 7.7 per cent in 2014 to 6.4 per cent in 2015 in North Africa, while it increased marginally, from 25.3 per cent in 2014 to 26.1 per cent in 2015, in

SDG 2 TARGETS	AGENDA 2063 GOALS 1, 3, 4, 5, 7 AND 8* TARGETS
2.1 By 2030, end hunger and ensure access by all people, in particular the poor and people in vulnerable situations, including infants, to safe, nutritious and sufficient food all year round	**1.1.2.4** Reduce 2013 levels of proportion of the population who suffer from hunger by at least 80%
	1.1.2.4 Reduce 2013 levels of proportion of the population who suffer from hunger by at least 80%
	1.5.1.9 End Hunger in Africa
2.2 By 2030, end all forms of malnutrition, including achieving, by 2025, the internationally agreed targets on stunting and wasting in children under 5 years of age, and address the nutritional needs of adolescent girls, pregnant and lactating women and older persons	**1.1.2.4** Reduce 2013 levels of proportion of the population who suffer from hunger by at least 80%
	1.1.2.5 Reduce stunting in children to 10% and underweight to 5%.
	1.3.1.7 Reduce 2013 level of prevalence of malnutrition by at least 50%
	1.3.1.8 Reduce stunting to 10%
	1.5.1.9 End Hunger in Africa
	1.5.1.10 Elimination of Child under nutrition with a view to bring down stunting to 10% and underweight to 5%
2.3 By 2030, double the agricultural productivity and incomes of small-scale food producers, in particular women, indigenous peoples, family farmers, pastoralists and fishers, including through secure and equal access to land, other productive resources and inputs, knowledge, financial services, markets and opportunities for value addition and non-farm employment	**1.5.1.2** Double agricultural total factor productivity
	1.5.1.3 Increase youth and women participation in integrated agricultural value chains by at least 30%
2.4 By 2030, ensure sustainable food production systems and implement resilient agricultural practices that increase productivity and production, that help maintain ecosystems, that strengthen capacity for adaptation to climate change, extreme weather, drought, flooding and other disasters and that progressively improve land and soil quality	**1.5.1.5** Increase the proportion of farm, pastoral and fisher households are resilient to climate and weather related risks to 30%
	17.1.2 At least 17% of terrestrial and inland water and 10% of coastal and marine areas are preserved
	1.7.2.2 Increase 2013 levels of water productivity from rain-fed agriculture and irrigation by 60%
	1.7.3.1 At least 30% of agricultural land is placed under sustainable land management practice
2.5 By 2020, maintain the genetic diversity of seeds, cultivated plants and farmed and domesticated animals and their related wild species, including through soundly managed and diversified seed and plant banks at the national, regional and international levels, and promote access to and fair and equitable sharing of benefits arising from the utilization of genetic resources and associated traditional knowledge, as internationally agreed	**1.7.1.4** Genetic diversity of cultivated plants and farmed and domesticated animals and of wild relatives including other socio-economically as well as cultural valuables species are maintained

SDG 2 TARGETS	AGENDA 2063 GOALS 1, 3, 4, 5, 7 AND 8* TARGETS
2.a Increase investment, including through enhanced international cooperation, in rural infrastructure, agricultural research and extension services, technology development and plant and livestock gene banks in order to enhance agricultural productive capacity in developing countries, in particular least developed countries	**1.5.1.1** Allocate a minimum of 10% annual public expenditure to agriculture and grow the sector by at least 6% per annum
	1.5.1.2 Double agricultural total factor productivity
	1.7.1.4 Genetic diversity of cultivated plants and farmed and domesticated animals and of wild relatives including other socio-economically as well as cultural valuables species are maintained
2.b Correct and prevent trade restrictions and distortions in world agricultural markets, including through the parallel elimination of all forms of agricultural export subsidies and all export measures with equivalent effect, in accordance with the mandate of the Doha Development Round	**2.8.1.1** Free movement of persons and goods/services within REC member states is in place
	2.8.1.3 Opportunities offered to REC citizens extended to other Non REC citizens
	2.8.1.5 Volume of intra-African trade is at least three times the 2013 level
	1.4.3.2 Reduce 2013 level of food imports by at least 50%.
	1.4.3.4 Level of intra-African trade in agricultural commodities is increased by at least 100% in real terms.
	1.5.1.8 Triple intra African Trade of agricultural commodities and services
	2.8.1.6 Volume of trade with African Island States is increased by at least 10%
2.c Adopt measures to ensure the proper functioning of food commodity markets and their derivatives and facilitate timely access to market information, including on food reserves, in order to help limit extreme food price volatility	**1.4.2.4** At least 5 commodity exchanges are functional

Source: Authors' own analysis based on Statistics Division (2017b) and African Union Commission (2015).

* Goal 1 (a high standard of living, quality of life and well-being for all), goal 3 (healthy and well-nourished citizens); goal 4 (transformed economies and job creation); goal 5 (modern agriculture for increased productivity and production) and goal 7 (environmentally sustainable climate-resilient economies and communities) of aspiration 1; and goal 8 (united Africa (federal or confederate) of aspiration 2.

Africa is making significant progress in several areas relating to hunger and food security, but remains fragile to shocks and is well below its potential for food production as reflected by the progress made in other regions of the world.

the rest of Africa. Second, agriculture, notwithstanding the commitments made for targeted investment under the Maputo Protocol, remains highly underinvested. None of the subregions has been able to achieve the target of allocating 10 per cent of the national budget to agriculture. Given the role of agriculture in reducing hunger and food insecurity, it is imperative that proactive measures be taken to increase agricultural productivity through investment in research and development, the irrigation of agricultural land, the development of value chains and putting in place investor-friendly rules and regulations. Lastly, data requirements for the proper monitoring of the Sustainable Development Goals are huge and the data gaps remain high. There is an urgent need to invest more financial and human resources as well as investing in new technologies to generate and disseminate data at all levels to enable efficient monitoring.

3.3 Progress and trends regarding the targets

The progress made by Africa on achieving Sustainable Development Goal 2 is mixed. Notable progress has been made in reducing hunger, but more needs to be done to catch up with the rest of the world. Progress in reducing food insecurity has been slow, with prevalence rates deteriorating slightly in 2015. Agricultural labour productivity in Africa (excluding North Africa) increased by 9 per cent during the period 2010-2015 and exceeded that of South Asia by 2010, but it is still well below the world average and most other regions. Africa's (excluding North Africa) agricultural value added per worker was 74 per cent that of Asia and the Pacific, 62 per cent of the world average and only 17 per cent that of Latin America and the Caribbean. Africa has not done well in irrigating agricultural land, a key underlying reason for low productivity. Irrigated agricultural land as a percentage of total agricultural land was only 5 per cent in Africa in 2010, compared with 41 per cent in Asia and 21 per cent globally.

Notwithstanding its importance in employment generation and food security, investment in agriculture has been very low in Africa. In fact, public investment in

Notable progress has been made in reducing hunger, but more needs to be done to catch up with the rest of the world.

agriculture declined gradually in Africa (excluding North Africa), more than the global average, over the years. The share of agriculture in government expenditure as a percentage of the share of agriculture in GDP dropped from 0.25 in 2001 to 0.14 in 2013 in Africa (excluding North Africa), indicating significant underfunding of the sector and reflecting the challenges in meeting the Maputo Protocol target of 10 per cent budgetary allocation to agriculture.

The flow of ODA to agriculture in all developing countries and least developed countries has been on an increasing trend since 2010, but current flows are less than half of what it received in the 1980s. Reflecting

BOX 3.2 EL NIÑO EFFECTS THREATEN AFRICA'S FOOD SECURITY

Africa has been facing one of its worst food crises, with the onset of the effects of El Niño, since early 2015 (World Food Programme, 2015), while El Niño-like impacts were felt in the Sahel, affecting, in particular, Mauritania and Senegal, which experienced their worst droughts in two decades. The most recent effects were seen in the Horn of Africa, in particular in Ethiopia and Somalia, and most countries in Southern Africa, but more so in Zimbabwe. In Ethiopia, 10.2 million people were food insecure in early 2016 (Food and Agriculture Organization of the United Nations, 2016), tripling the humanitarian needs within a year owing to successive crop failures and widespread livestock deaths. Similar conditions were seen in Somalia and South Sudan, affecting an estimated 7.5 million people. Most Southern African countries were also affected by the effects in the latter part of 2015, with the worst severe drought conditions in decades witnessed in Madagascar, Malawi, South Africa, Swaziland and Zimbabwe. Almost 40 million people were affected.

The effects of El Niño throughout Africa points to several policy issues. First, large-scale humanitarian support is required to assist food-insecure populations, institutional arrangements and coordination. Second, they highlight the need for all countries to be well prepared for such emergencies, including through strengthening climate-smart agricultural practices, investing in irrigation and building emergency food reserves. Third, adaptation to climate effects and taking proactive steps to mitigate human contributions to climate change could go a long way to addressing climate-related disasters in the long run. Lastly, sustained and sustainable economic development could always act as a buffer to such crises by providing the resources required to affected populations from within to build greater resilience to shocks.

these trends, the flow of ODA to agriculture in Africa (excluding North Africa) declined from a peak of approximately 25 per cent in the early 1980s to approximately 6 per cent by 2007. Meanwhile, there has been a noticeable drop in agricultural export subsidies.

Target 2.1 of Sustainable Development Goal 2

By 2030, end hunger and ensure access by all people, in particular the poor and people in vulnerable situation, including infants, to safe, nutritious and sufficient food all year round

Related Agenda 2063 targets:

i   Reduce the 2013 levels of proportion of the population who suffer from hunger by at least 80 per cent;

ii   End hunger in Africa.

This target has two indicators under Sustainable Development Goal 2: 2.1.1 (prevalence of undernourishment) and 2.1.2 (estimated prevalence of moderate or severe food insecurity in the adult population). The related indicators under Agenda 2063 include (a) end hunger in Africa; (b) the share of population living below minimal level of daily dietary energy; and (c) reduce 2013 levels of proportion of the population who suffer from hunger by at least 80 per cent.

Overall, Africa has made notable progress in reducing hunger over the years. For example, the prevalence of undernourishment in North Africa remained low, at below 5 per cent, from 2000 to 2016, while it dropped from 30 to 22.9 per cent during the same period in the rest of Africa (see TABLE 3.2). Nevertheless, hunger remained much higher in Africa (excluding North Africa) compared with all other regions. The prevalence of undernourishment in Africa (excluding North Africa) during the period 2014-2016 was twice as high as the global average of 10.8 per cent, a condition that has prevailed during the past several decades. During the periods 2010-2012 and 2014-2016, the prevalence of undernourishment declined sharply in the Caucasus and Central Asia (21 per cent), South East Asia (20 per

Food insecurity and undernourishment are binding constraints to development in Africa and require sustained policy attention.

TABLE 3.2   GLOBAL PREVALENCE OF UNDERNOURISHMENT BY REGION

(PER CENT)

REGION	2000-02	2005-07	2010-12	2014-16
World	14.9	14.3	11.8	10.8
Developing regions	18.2	17.3	14.1	12.9
North Africa	<5.0	<5.0	<5.0	<5.0
Africa (excluding North Africa)	30.0	26.5	24.2	22.9
Latin America and the Caribbean	11.4	8.4	6.4	5.5
East Asia	16.0	15.2	11.8	9.6
South Asia	18.5	20.1	16.1	15.7
South East Asia	22.3	18.3	12.1	9.6
Western Asia	8.6	9.3	8.9	8.4
Oceania	16.5	15.4	13.5	14.2
Caucasus and Central Asia	15.3	11.3	8.9	7.0
Developed regions	<5.0	<5.0	<5.0	<5.0

Source: Statistics Division (2016).

cent), East Asia (18 per cent) and Latin America and the Caribbean (14 per cent), compared with a drop of 5 per cent in Africa (excluding North Africa).

Meanwhile, moderate or severe food insecurity remained high in Africa (excluding North Africa), with the prevalence rate increasing moderately, from 54.3 per cent in 2014 to 57.2 per cent in 2015, while that in North Africa fell from 21.8 to 18.6 per cent during the same period (see FIGURE 3.1). The effects of El Niño on the African continent, in particular in the Horn of Africa (especially Ethiopia) and Southern Africa, have contributed to the deteriorating food insecurity in the region. The number of people undernourished in Africa (excluding North Africa), estimated to be 217 million during the period 2014-2016, reflected an increase of 6 per cent compared with the period 2010-2012. Ethiopia, Nigeria, Uganda and the United Republic of Tanzania, having 31.6, 12.9, 10.3 and 16.8 million undernourished populations, respectively, accounted for one third of the total undernourished population in Africa (excluding North Africa). Some 355 million people in Africa were moderately or severely food insecure in 2015, compared with a marginal increase in moderate or severe food insecurity globally and a

modest increase in Latin America, South East Asia and Western Asia.

The prevalence of severe food insecurity also increased marginally, from 25.3 per cent in 2014 to 26.1 per cent in 2015 in Africa (excluding North Africa), while in North Africa it declined from 7.7 per cent to 6.4 per cent (see FIGURE 3.1). These figures compare with no change in the prevalence of severe food insecurity globally, a significant deterioration in South East Asia, with an increase of 24 per cent, and a moderate increase, of 5.3 per cent, in Western Asia. A total of 161 million people in Africa were severely food insecure in 2015. By far, the majority of them, or 96 per cent, were from rural areas. Underlying these numbers are the economic slowdown (from 5.0 per cent in 2014 to 3.4 per cent in 2015 and an estimated 1.6 per cent in 2016) and the drought experienced by many African countries (International Monetary Fund, 2015; 2016).

The above analysis points to key challenges in relation to food security and undernourishment. Food insecurity and undernourishment are binding constraints to development in Africa and require sustained policy attention.

FIGURE 3.1   ESTIMATED PREVALENCE OF MODERATE OR SEVERE FOOD INSECURITY IN THE ADULT POPULATION

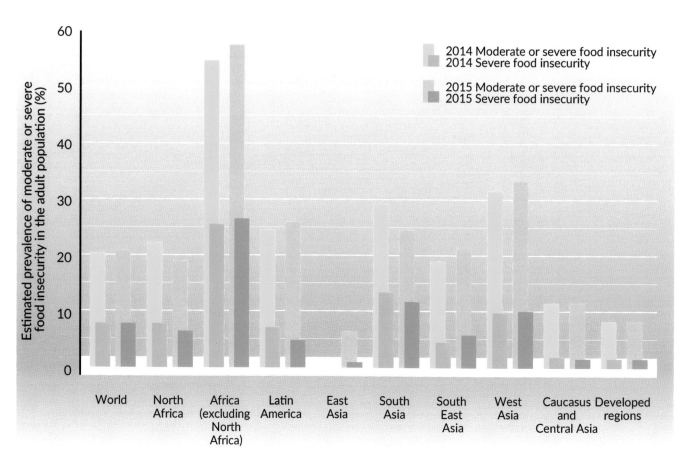

Source: Statistics Division (2016).   Note: estimates computed using the Food Insecurity Experience Scale.

Target 2.2 of Sustainable Development Goal 2
By 2030, end all forms of malnutrition, including achieving, by 2025, the internationally agreed targets on stunting and wasting in children under 5 years of age, and address the nutritional needs of adolescent girls, pregnant and lactating women and older persons

Related Agenda 2063 targets:

i   Reduce stunting in children to 10 per cent and underweight to 5 per cent;

ii   Reduce stunting to 10 per cent;

iii   End hunger in Africa.

This target has two indicators: 2.2.1 (prevalence of stunting[1]) and 2.2.2 (proportion of children under 5 years of age with WHZ <-2). The related indicators under Agenda 2063 include prevalence of stunting among children under 5 years of age and prevalence of underweight among children under 5 years of age.

Africa made some progress in reducing malnutrition between 2000 and 2014, but at a rate much lower than other regions. As indicated in TABLE 3.3, the proportion of children under 5 years of age whose height for age is below two standard deviations from the median of the child growth standards of the World Health Organization (WHO) (HAZ <-2) was at 35.7 per cent, second only to Oceania (38.9 per cent). The prevalence of stunting dropped by 17.3 per cent in Africa (excluding North Africa), while that in North Africa declined by 25.7 per cent, compared with a reduction of 27.2 per cent at the global level, 66 per cent in East Asia, 43.1 per cent in Caucasus and Central Asia and 36.5 per cent in Latin America and the Caribbean. Only in Oceania did the prevalence of stunting increase (from 37.6 per cent in 2000 to 38.9 per cent, the highest in the world, in 2014). The number of stunted children under 5 years of age in Africa (excluding North Africa) stood at 57.3 million in 2014, reflecting an increase from 55.8 million in 2010 and 50.1 million in 2000. Stunting is an issue that has not received serious attention, especially in Africa. The primary cause of stunting is the insufficient intake of calories and micronutrients to support the

---

1   Stunting is defined as when height for age <-2 standard deviation from the median of the World Health Organization child growth standards) among children under 5 years of age.

REGION	2000	2005	2010	2014
World	32.7	29.4	26.2	23.8
Developing regions	36.0	32.3	28.8	26.0
North Africa	24.1	21.7	19.6	17.9
Africa (excluding North Africa)	43.2	40.5	37.8	35.7
Latin America and the Caribbean	16.7	14.2	12.1	10.6
East Asia	19.1	13.2	9.0	6.5
South Asia	49.5	44.3	39.3	35.4
South East Asia	38.3	34.2	30.2	27.3
Western Asia	23.6	20.9	18.5	16.7
Oceania	37.6	38.1	38.6	38.9
Caucasus and Central Asia	26.9	22.2	18.1	15.3
Developed regions	4.8	4.6	4.4	4.2

* HAZ<-2 refers to chronic malnutrition among children between 0 and 59 months of age whose height for age is below the minus two standard deviations from the median of the child growth standards of the World Health Organization.

Source: Statistics Division (2017).

normal growth of a child. Underlying this are issues relating to environmental and economic conditions, such as poor air quality, infections from poor sanitation and limited access to nutritious food.

The proportion of children under 5 years of age whose weight for height is below two standard deviations from the median of the WHO child growth standards (WHZ <-2) stood at 8.3 per cent in Africa (excluding North Africa) and 7.3 per cent in North Africa in 2014 (see FIGURE 3.2). This is slightly above the global average of 7.5 per cent, well above Latin America and the Caribbean (1.3 per cent), East Asia (2.1 per cent) Western Asia (4 per cent) and Caucasus and Central Asia (3.9 per cent), but well below South Asia (14.2 per cent).

FIGURE 3.2 CHILDREN UNDER 5 YEARS OF AGE WITH WHZ<-2, 2014

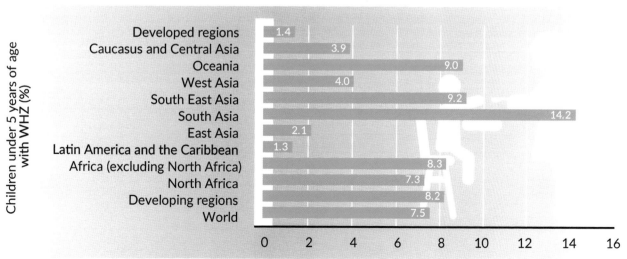

Note: WHZ<-2 refers to children between 0 and 59 months of age whose weight for height is below the minus two standard deviations from the median of the World Health Organization child growth standards.
Source: Statistics Division (2016).

The proportion of overweight children in Africa (excluding North Africa) remained at 4.5 per cent in 2014. Overweight is a specific issue among children in North Africa, where the proportion of overweight children increased from 12.2 per cent in 2000 and 13.5 per cent in 2005 to 14.9 per cent in 2010.

Child stunting is a major challenge to the continent's human capital in Africa because of its life-long implications on brain development. Improving nutritious food intake among children under five years of age, including through improved food production and distribution and better sanitation and environmental conditions, is critical to reducing stunting in the region.

Target 2.3 of Sustainable Development Goal 2

By 2030, double the agricultural productivity and incomes of small-scale food producers, in particular women, indigenous peoples, family farmers, pastoralists and fishers, including through secure and equal access to land, other productive resources and inputs, knowledge, financial services, markets and opportunities for value addition and non-farm employment

Related Agenda 2063 targets:

i   Double agricultural total factor productivity;

ii   Increase the participation of young people and women in integrated agricultural value chains by at least 30 per cent.

Agricultural labour productivity in Africa (excluding North Africa) increased by 9 per cent during the period 2010-2015 and exceeded that of South Asia by 2010. However, agricultural labour productivity in Africa (excluding North Africa) is well below the rest of the world.

This target has one indicator: 2.3.1 (volume of production per labour unit by classes of farming/pastoral/forestry enterprise size). Related indicators under Agenda 2063 include agricultural total productivity doubled and proportion of reduction of post-harvest losses and percentage growth of agricultural GDP produced by commercial farmers.

Agricultural labour productivity in Africa (excluding North Africa) increased by 9 per cent during the period 2010-2015 and exceeded that of South Asia by 2010. However, agricultural labour productivity in Africa (excluding North Africa) is well below the rest of the world. For example, agricultural value added per worker in Africa (excluding North Africa), at constant 2010 $1,221, was below the world average of $1,978, and $1,657 for Asia and the Pacific in 2015 (see TABLE 3.4). It is well below the averages for Latin America and the Caribbean ($7,140) and high-income countries (approximately $30,000). The rest of Africa's agricultural value added per worker was 74 per cent that of Asia and the Pacific, 62 per cent of the world average and 17 per cent that of Latin America and the Caribbean. Its labour productivity is only 4 per cent that of high-income countries.

Greater investment is needed to improve agricultural productivity in Africa. Technological applications, irrigation, water management and agro-processing are some of the areas that Africa may need to focus on in order to improve agricultural productivity and, hence, regional food security.

Target 2.4 of Sustainable Development Goal 2

By 2030, ensure sustainable food production systems and implement resilient agricultural practices that increase productivity and production, that help to maintain ecosystems, that strengthen capacity for adaptation to climate change, extreme weather, drought, flooding and other disasters and that progressively improve land and soil quality

Related Agenda 2063 targets:

i   Increase the proportion of farm, pastoral and fisher households that are resilient to climate-related and weather-related risks to 30 per cent;

ii   At least 30 per cent of agricultural land is placed under sustainable land management practice;

REGION	2010	2015	SHARE AS PERCENTAGE OF HIGH-INCOME COUNTRIES (2015)	RATIO OF AFRICA (EXCLUDING NORTH AFRICA) TO OTHER REGIONS (2015)
World	1,944.8	1,978.3	6.60	0.62
Africa (excluding North Africa)	1,121.2	1,221.6	4.07	1.00
Latin America and the Caribbean	6,410.1	7,139.9	23.81	0.17
East Asia and the Pacific	1,464.3	1,656.9	5.53	0.74
South Asia	1,048.5	1,124.5	3.75	1.09
High-income countries	31,899.8	29,982.9	100.00	0.04

Source: World Bank world development indicators (2016).

iii   At least 17 per cent of terrestrial and inland water and 10 per cent of coastal and marine areas are preserved;

iv   Increase 2013 levels of water productivity from rain-fed agriculture and irrigation by 60 per cent.

This target has one indicator: 2.4.1 (percentage of agricultural area under sustainable agricultural practices). Related indicators under Agenda 2063 include: (a) proportion of pastoral and fisher households that are resilient to climate-related and weather-related risk; (b) proportion of agricultural land placed under sustainable land management practice; (c) proportion of terrestrial and inland water areas and of coastal and marine areas preserved; and (d) proportion of water productivity used in rain-fed agriculture and irrigation.

Progress here remains limited, and further public and private sector investment is required for Africa to benefit from its huge agricultural potential, increase its capacity to feed its people and expand export revenue. As of 2010, agricultural irrigated land as a percentage of total agricultural land was only 5 per cent in Africa, compared with 41 per cent in Asia and 21 per cent at the global level (see FIGURE 3.3). This implies that the bulk of agricultural production in Africa is rain-fed, which is unsustainable, given the increasing population and consequent demand for food. With climate change and rainfall patterns changing, investment in irrigation is required to ensure sustainable food production and increased factor productivity.

FIGURE 3.3 AGRICULTURAL IRRIGATED LAND AS PERCENTAGE OF TOTAL AGRICULTURAL LAND

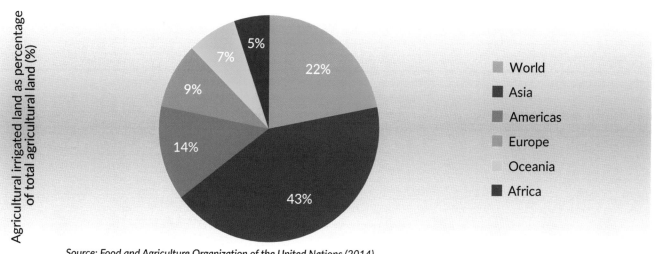

Source: Food and Agriculture Organization of the United Nations (2014).

Target 2.5 of Sustainable Development Goal 2

By 2020, maintain the genetic diversity of seeds, cultivated plants and farmed and domesticated animals and their related wild species, including through soundly managed and diversified see and plant banks at the national, regional and international levels, and promote access to and fair and equitable sharing of benefits arising from the utilization of genetic resources and associated traditional knowledge, as internationally agreed

Related Agenda 2063 target:

i   Genetic diversity of cultivated plants and farmed and domesticated animals and of wild relatives, including other socioeconomically and culturally valuable species, is maintained.

This target has one indicator: 2.5.2 (proportion of local breeds classified as being at risk, not-at-risk or at unknown). Agenda 2063 also has one indicator: diversity index (proportion of genetic diversity of cultivated plants and farmed and domesticated animals and of wild rela-

tives, including other socioeconomically and culturally valuables species, is maintained).

In Africa, the known level of risk of extinction of local breeds remains moderate, compared with other regions of the world. For example, the proportion of local breeds classified as being at risk is 1.9 per cent for Africa (excluding North Africa), compared with 19.7 per cent at the global level. This is still higher than South Asia (0.4 per cent) and Latin America and the Caribbean (1.5 per cent). However, it is lower than Western Asia (5.4 per cent) and East Asia (4.2 per cent). The share of local breeds not at risk, at 9.3 per cent in Africa (excluding North Africa), is higher only than that of Latin America and the Caribbean (3 per cent). The level risk of extinction classified as "unknown" accounts for

TABLE 3.5 LEVEL OF RISK OF EXTINCTION OF LOCAL BREEDS, BY REGION

(PER CENT)

REGION	NOT AT RISK*	AT RISK*	UNKNOWN**
World	15.6	19.7	64.7
Developing regions	11.6	2.1	89.3
North Africa	0	0	100
Africa (excluding North Africa)	9.3	1.9	88.8
Latin America and the Caribbean	3.0	1.5	95.5
East Asia	24.5	4.2	71.3
South Asia	13.2	0.4	86.5
South-East Asia	17.9	2.6	79.5
Western Asia	9.4	5.4	85.2
Oceania	0	0	100
Caucasus and Central Asia	0	0	100
Developed regions	19.7	37.4	42.9

Source: Statistics Division (2016).

* Data for "at-risk" and "not at-risk" status are fewer than 10 years old.

** "Unknown" status means that no updates have been received on the population sizes at least in the past 10 years.

a large share, 65 per cent at the global level and 100 per cent in some regions, the actual risk of extinction may be much higher than recorded for most regions (see TABLE 3.5)

Target 2.a of Sustainable Development Goal 2:

Increase investment, including through enhanced international cooperation, in rural infrastructure, agricultural research and extension services, technology development and plant and livestock gene banks in order to enhance agricultural productive capacity in developing countries, in particular least developed countries

Related Agenda 2063 targets:

i   Allocate a minimum of 10 per cent annual public expenditure to agriculture and grow the sector by at least 6 per cent annually;

ii   Double agricultural total factor productivity;

iii Genetic diversity of cultivated plants and farmed and domesticated animals and of wild relatives, including other socioeconomically and culturally valuable species, is maintained.

This target has two indicators: 2.a.1 (the agriculture orientation index for government expenditure) and 2.a.2 (total official flows (ODA plus other official flows) to the agriculture sector).

Agenda 2063 has four related indicators: (a) proportion of annual allocation of budget to the agriculture sector; (b) percentage contribution of the agriculture sector to GDP; (c) agricultural total production and productivity doubled; and (d) diversity index (percentage of genetic diversity of cultivated plants and farmed and domesticated animals and of wild relatives, including other socioeconomically and culturally valuable species, maintained).

One of the indicators used to assess the progress made in investing in agriculture is the "agricultural orientation index", which reflects the extent to which government expenditure on agriculture mirrors (or not) the importance of agriculture in the overall economy. Notwithstanding its importance in employment generation and food security, investment in agriculture has declined gradually in Africa (excluding North Africa). The index for government expenditure dropped from 0.25 in 2001 and 0.18 in 2010 and to 0.14 in 2013

TABLE 3.6   AGRICULTURE ORIENTATION INDEX OF GOVERNMENT EXPENDITURE *

REGION	2001	2005	2010	2013
World	0.37	0.35	0.25	0.25
Developing regions	0.37	0.35	0.35	0.33
North Africa	1.05	0.26	0.14	0.14
Africa (excluding North Africa)	0.25	0.25	0.18	0.14
Latin America and the Caribbean	0.26	0.21	0.34	0.22
East Asia	1.53	1.58	0.39	0.37
South Asia	0.2	0.27	0.38	0.33
South-East Asia	0.52	0.33	0.24	0.29
Western Asia	0.34	1.09	0.47	0.66
Oceania		0.24	0.19	0.16
Caucasus and Central Asia	0.13	0.48	0.73	0.57
Developed regions	0.49	0.53	0.42	0.41

Source: Statistics Division (2016).

* The agriculture orientation index for government expenditure is defined as the agriculture share of government expenditure divided by the agriculture share of GDP. Agriculture refers to the agriculture, forestry, fishing and hunting sectors.

in Africa (excluding North Africa), while at the global level it declined from 0.37 in 2001 to 0.25 in 2013 (see TABLE 3.6). The regions that saw an increase in the index are the Caucasus and Central Asia (338 per cent), Western Asia (94 per cent) and South Asia (65 per cent). North Africa registered the largest drop in the index (87 per cent), indicating declining public investment in agriculture.

The current level of public investment in agriculture indicates large gaps in meeting one of the prominent commitments made in the Maputo Protocol, calling for African governments to allocate 10 per cent of budgetary resources to agriculture and rural development policy implementation within five years, that is, by 2008. To date, none of Africa's subregions has met this commitment and the level of investment has been erratic, with some regions progressing while others have regressed. The highest level of investment in agriculture has been reached by East Africa, at 5.8 per cent of total public expenditure (see FIGURE 3.4).

The second indicator used to assess the progress made in investing in agriculture is the total annual flow of ODA to agriculture. Historically, agriculture has received the least amount of ODA. For example, since the mid-1980s, aid to agriculture has fallen by 43 per cent, but the rate of decline has slowed down in recent years. The share of ODA to agriculture by Development Assistance Committee members dropped even more sharply, to 6 per cent by 2003 (Organization for Economic Cooperation and Development, 2010). A similar trend is seen in ODA flows to agriculture in Africa (excluding North Africa), which declined from a peak of approximately 25 per cent in the early 1980s to approximately 6 per cent by 2007 (Food and Agriculture Organization of the United Nations, 2009). As indicated in TABLE 3.7, ODA to agriculture in all developing countries and least developed countries has increased since 2010, but they have received less than half of what they received in the 1980s. Moreover, ODA flows to agriculture in landlocked countries and small island developing States dropped even further.

Further public and private sector investment is required for Africa to benefit from its huge agricultural potential, increase its capacity to feed its people and expand export revenue.

FIGURE 3.4 ANNUAL AGRICULTURE SHARE IN TOTAL PUBLIC EXPENDITURE

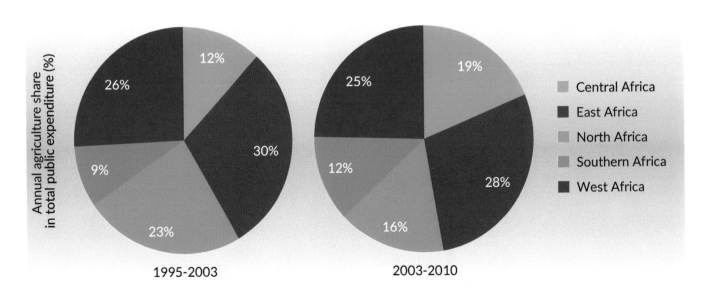

Source: Regional Strategy Analysis and Knowledge Support System.

TABLE 3.7 TOTAL OFFICIAL DISBURSEMENTS FOR AGRICULTURE (BILLIONS OF CONSTANT 2014 UNITED STATES DOLLARS)

	2000	2005	2010	2014
All developing countries	9.37	5.73	11.98	12.1
Least developed countries	3.40	1.79	3.66	3.89
Landlocked developing countries	2.94	1.33	2.76	2.65
Small island developing States	0.65	0.14	0.42	0.29

Source: Statistics Division (2016)

Target 2.b of Sustainable Development Goal 2

Correct and prevent trade restrictions and distortions in world agricultural markets, including through the parallel elimination of all forms of agricultural export subsidies and all export measures with equivalent effect, in accordance with the mandate of the Doha Development Round

Related Agenda 2063 targets:

i Reduce the 2013 level of food imports by at least 50 per cent;

ii Level of intra-African trade in agricultural commodities is increased by at least 100 per cent in real terms;

iii Triple intra-African trade in agricultural commodities and services;

iv Free movement of persons and goods/services within regional economic commission member States is in place;

v Volume of intra-African trade is at least three times the 2013 level.

This target has two indicators: 2.b.1 (producer support) and 2.b.2 (agricultural export subsidies).

Related indicators under Agenda 2063 include: (a) percentage of food imported; (b) percentage increase in intra-Africa trade in agricultural commodities; (c) volume of intra- Africa trade in agricultural commodities and services in place; (d) number of obstacles on the free movement of persons and goods and services reported; (e) percentage of opportunities offered to regional economic commission citizens extended to non-regional economic commission citizens; (f) rate of increase in annual intra-African trade volume; and (g) rate of increase in volume of annual trade with African island States.

While producer support in the agricultural sector has increased significantly at the global level, it declined marginally in countries of the Organization for Economic Cooperation and Development (OECD). For example, estimates indicate that producer support at the global level more than doubled, from $258 billion in 2000 to $584 million in 2014. Of that total, the share of OECD support declined from 95 per cent ($244 million) to 40 per cent ($239 million) during the same period (see TABLE 3.8).

Many countries have voluntarily removed agriculture export subsidies owing to prevailing high commodity prices, and only a handful of member countries of the World Trade Organization (WTO) still use agri-

TABLE 3.8 PRODUCER SUPPORT ESTIMATE (BILLIONS OF UNITED STATES DOLLARS)

	2000	2005	2010	2014
World*	258	318	440	584
Countries of the Organization for Economic Cooperation and Development	244	266	247	239

* Producer support estimates cover Organization for Economic Cooperation and Development and emerging economies that, together, account for approximately 88 per cent of global value added in agriculture.

Source: Statistics Division (2016).

TABLE 3.9 AGRICULTURAL EXPORT SUBSIDIES

(BILLIONS OF UNITED STATES DOLLARS)

	2000	2005	2010	2014
All members of the World Trade Organization	2.97	2.72	0.46	0.11
Developing members of the World Trade Organization	0.1	0.08	0.02	0.002
Developed members of the World Trade Organization	2.89	2.64	0.43	0.1

Note: Notifications by World Trade Organization member States under the Agreement on Agriculture. The notification record varies from year to year, and therefore the set of countries represented in the data may differ among the years reported, in particular in more recent periods.

Source: Statistics Division (2016).

culture export subsidies (World Trade Organization, 2015). The declining trend in export subsidies was followed by a further commitment by WTO members at its tenth ministerial meeting in Nairobi in 2015 to abolish agriculture export subsidies.

Agricultural export subsidies, the majority of which have been issued by developed countries, declined significantly, from almost $3 billion to almost zero by 2014 (see TABLE 3.9).[2]

---

2 Please note that reported export subsidies may not fully capture all export subsidies such as those not covered by budgetary expenditure.

3.4 Conclusion

Africa's progress towards achieving Sustainable Development Goal 2 is mixed. The continent has made significant progress in some of the targets under the Goal, while, in others, progress has been slow. Significant achievements have been made in reducing hunger. The prevalence of undernourishment dropped from 30 per cent in 2000 to 22.9 per cent in 2016 in Africa (excluding North Africa), while that in North Africa remained low, at below 5 per cent during that period. Notwithstanding a drop in the prevalence of stunting by 17.3 per cent in Africa (excluding North Africa) and by 25.7 per cent in North Africa, stunting remained high, at 35.7 per cent, second only to Oceania (38.9 per cent). The prevalence of moderate or severe food insecurity and severe food insecurity remained high in Africa (excluding North Africa), with the prevalence rates increasing from 54.3 per cent in 2014 to 57.2 per cent in 2015 and from 25.3 per cent in 2014 to 26.1 per cent, respectively. Altogether, some 355 million people in Africa were moderately or severely food insecure in 2015. The number of people undernourished in Africa (excluding North Africa), recorded at 217 million during the period 2014-2016, reflected an increase of 6 per cent, compared with the period 2010-2012.

Agricultural labour productivity in Africa (excluding North Africa) increased significantly (57 per cent), the highest in the world during the period 2000-2015, but it is still well below the world average and most other regions. Agricultural productivity growth has moderated since 2005, although some gains have been made more recently. Irrigated agricultural land as a percentage of total agricultural land was only 5 per cent in Africa, compared with 41 per cent in Asia and 21 per cent globally, one of the underlying reasons for low productivity. Agricultural value added per worker in Africa (excluding North Africa) at constant 2010 $1,221 is below the world average of $1,978 and $1,657 for Asia and the

The continent has made significant progress in some of the targets under the Goal, while, in others, progress has been slow.

Key challenges in achieving the Sustainable Development Goals include addressing food security and undernourishment. Doing so will require greater investment in agriculture and increased agricultural productivity, including through higher levels of irrigation, technology and value addition.

Pacific. Public investment in agriculture declined gradually in Africa (excluding North Africa), more than the global average, over the years, while the flow of ODA to agriculture declined from a peak of approximately 25 per cent in the early 1980s to approximately 6 per cent by 2007. In addition, there has been a noticeable drop in agricultural export subsidies.

Key challenges in achieving the Sustainable Development Goals include addressing food security and undernourishment. Doing so will require greater investment in agriculture and increased agricultural productivity, including through higher levels of irrigation, technology and value addition. Commitments made in the Maputo Protocol to allocate 10 per cent of national budgets to agriculture and rural development policy should inspire the achievement of this goal. Building resilience to shocks, including through adaptation to the effects of climate change, strengthening institutional response mechanisms and sustained and sustainable development, will provide space for countries to deal with disasters better and address food security. Data requirements for the proper monitoring of the Goals is huge, and the analysis reveals the large gaps in data requirements. There is an urgent need to invest more in generating and disseminating data at all levels to enable efficient monitoring.

CHAPTER 4

Sustainable Development Goal 3: Good health and well-being

4.1 Introduction

Sustainable Development Goal 3 of the 2030 Agenda, to ensure healthy lives and promote well-being for all at all ages, addresses all major health priorities, including reproductive, maternal and child health; communicable, non-communicable and environmental diseases; universal health coverage; and access for all to safe, effective, quality and affordable medicines and vaccines. It also contains calls for more research and development, increased health financing and the strengthened capacity of all countries in health risk reduction and management. Agenda 2063 also contains goals that seek to ensure healthy and well-nourished citizens. There is therefore a high degree of convergence between both Agendas.

Health is strongly linked to other sustainable development goals. It is influenced by environmental issues and by socioeconomic factors, such as living conditions. Good health is also necessary for a person to be productive and have the resources to contribute to life. A healthy population also ensures added value for the economy and society.

Health is strongly linked to other sustainable development goals. It is influenced by environmental issues and by socioeconomic factors.

4.2 Targets and alignment with Agenda 2063

Sustainable Development Goal 3 has 13 targets with 21 indicators and is fully aligned with Agenda 2063's goal 3 (healthy and well-nourished citizens) and partially aligned with goal 17 (full gender equality in all spheres of life) (see TABLE 4.1).

SDG 3 TARGETS	AGENDA 2063 GOALS 3 AND 17* TARGETS
3.1 By 2030, reduce the global maternal mortality ratio to less than 70 per 100,000 live births	**1.3.1.3** Reduce 2013 maternal, neo-natal and child mortality rates by at least 50%
	6.17.2.3 Eliminate all barriers to quality education, health & social services for women & girls by 2020
	6.17.2.3 Eliminate all barriers to quality education, health and social services for Women and Girls by 2020
3.2 By 2030, end preventable deaths of newborns and children under 5 years of age, with all countries aiming to reduce neonatal mortality to at least as low as 12 per 1,000 live births and under-5 mortality to at least as low as 25 per 1,000 live births	**1.3.1.3** Reduce 2013 maternal, neo-natal and child mortality rates by at least 50%
3.3 By 2030, end the epidemics of AIDS, tuberculosis, malaria and neglected tropical diseases and combat hepatitis, water-borne diseases and other communicable diseases	**1.3.1.4** Reduce 2013 proportion of deaths attributable to HIV/AIDs, Malaria and TB by at least 50%
	1.3.1.5 Reduce under 5 mortality rate attributable to malaria by at least 80%
	1.3.1.6 Reduce the 2013 incidence of HIV/AIDs, Malaria and TB by at least 80%
	1.3.1.9 Reduce 2013 proportion of deaths attributable to dengue fever and chikungnya by 50% (for Island States)
3.4 By 2030, reduce by one third premature mortality from non-communicable diseases through prevention and treatment and promote mental health and well-being	
3.5 Strengthen the prevention and treatment of substance abuse, including narcotic drug abuse and harmful use of alcohol	
3.6 By 2020, halve the number of global deaths and injuries from road traffic accidents	
3.7 By 2030, ensure universal access to sexual and reproductive health-care services, including for family planning, information and education, and the integration of reproductive health into national strategies and programmes	**1.3.1.2** Increase 2013 levels of access to sexual and reproductive health services to women by at least 30%
3.8 Achieve universal health coverage, including financial risk protection, access to quality essential health-care services and access to safe, effective, quality and affordable essential medicines and vaccines for all	**1.3.1.1** Increase 2013 levels of access to quality basic health care and services by at least 40%
	1.3.1.10 Access to Anti-Retroviral (ARV) drugs is 100%
3.9 By 2030, substantially reduce the number of deaths and illnesses from hazardous chemicals and air, water and soil pollution and contamination	**1.7.3.3** Reduce deaths and property loss from natural and man-made disasters and climate extreme events by at least 30%

TABLE 4.1   (CONT)

SDG 3 TARGETS	AGENDA 2063 GOALS 3 AND 17* TARGETS
3.a Strengthen the implementation of the World Health Organization Framework Convention on Tobacco Control in all countries, as appropriate	
3.b Support the research and development of vaccines and medicines for the communicable and non-communicable diseases that primarily affect developing countries, provide access to affordable essential medicines and vaccines, in accordance with the Doha Declaration on the TRIPS Agreement and Public Health, which affirms the right of developing countries to use to the full the provisions in the Agreement on Trade-Related Aspects of Intellectual Property Rights regarding flexibilities to protect public health, and, in particular, provide access to medicines for all	**1.3.1.10** Access to Anti-Retroviral (ARV) drugs is 100%
3.c Substantially increase health financing and the recruitment, development, training and retention of the health workforce in developing countries, especially in least developed countries and small island developing States	
3.d Strengthen the capacity of all countries, in particular developing countries, for early warning, risk reduction and management of national and global health risks	

Source: Authors' own analysis based on Statistics Division (2017b) and African Union Commission (2015).

* Goal 3 (healthy and well-nourished citizens) of aspiration 1 and goal 17 (full gender equality in all spheres of life) of aspiration 6.

BOX 4.1 GLOBAL HEALTH STATUS: MOST RECENT OVERVIEW

During the period 1990-2015, the maternal mortality ratio declined by 44 per cent, and under-five child mortality fell by more than 50 per cent. An estimated 5.9 million children under 5 years of age died in 2015, mostly from preventable causes. The incidence of HIV, malaria and tuberculosis declined globally between 2000 and 2015. However, in 2015, 2.1 million people became newly infected with HIV and an estimated 214 million people contracted malaria. Approximately 50 per cent of the world's population is at risk of malaria, but Africa (excluding North Africa) accounted for 89 per cent of all cases in 2015. In 2015, approximately 75 per cent women of reproductive age (between 15 and 49 years) who were married or in a union satisfied their need for family planning by using modern contraceptive methods. In 2012, almost two thirds of deaths from non-communicable diseases in people under 70 years of age were attributed to cardiovascular diseases and cancer.

Source: United Nations (2016a).

4.3 Current status in Africa and the progress made

The present discussion focuses on seven of the most relevant targets of Sustainable Development Goal 3, namely 3.1 through 3.7, and defines the current status and trends along the specified indicator.

Target 3.1 of Sustainable Development Goal 3
By 2030, reduce the global maternal mortality ratio to less than 70 per 100,000 live births

Related Agenda 2063 target:

i   Reduce 2013 maternal, neonatal and child mortality rates by at least 50 per cent.

Indicator 3.1.1: maternal mortality ratio

Problems during pregnancy and childbirth are a leading cause of death and disability of women of reproductive age (between 15 and 49 years) in developing countries. This indicator acts as a record of deaths relating to pregnancy and childbirth and reflects the ability of a country's health-care system to provide safe care during pregnancy and childbirth.

The global maternal mortality ratio declined by 44 per cent between 1990 and 2015. Africa has also made remarkable progress in reducing maternal mortality over the years. The maternal mortality ratio dropped from 846 deaths per 100,000 live births in 2000 to 546 deaths per 100,000 live births in 2015 in Africa (excluding North Africa), while that North Africa remained low, at 70 deaths per 1000,000 as the target (see TABLE 4.2). The ratio remained higher, however, in Africa (excluding North Africa) compared with all other regions. In Africa and other developing regions, the risk

In Africa and other developing regions, the risk of a woman dying from a maternal cause is approximately 23 times higher than for a woman living in a developed country.

TABLE 4.2 MATERNAL MORTALITY RATIO BY REGION (DEATHS PER 100,000 LIVE BIRTHS)

REGION	2000	2005	2010	2015
World	341	288	246	216
Developing regions	377	319	273	239
North Africa	113	95	82	70
Africa (excluding North Africa)	846	717	624	546
Latin America and the Caribbean	99	88	81	67
East Asia	59	48	36	27
South Asia	377	288	221	176
South East Asia	201	166	136	110
Western Asia	122	110	96	91
Oceania	292	239	206	187
Caucasus and Central Asia	50	46	37	33
Developed regions	17	15	13	12

Source: Statistics Division (2016).

of a woman dying from a maternal cause is approximately 23 times higher than for a woman living in a developed country.

The maternal mortality ratio varies substantially throughout the African continent. Many African countries registered progress in reducing their maternal mortality ratio between 1990 and 2015. However, a significant number of African countries still have a very high maternal mortality ratio. Twenty African countries reported a maternal mortality ratio of more than 500 deaths per 100,000 live births in 2015 (Figure 4.1). Sierra Leone had the highest maternal mortality, at 1,360 deaths per 100,000 live births. Only five African countries, namely, Cabo Verde, Egypt, Libya, Mauritius and Tunisia, had a ratio below the Sustainable Development Goal target of 70 deaths per 100,000 live births. Through Agenda 2063, reducing 2013 maternal mortality rates by at least 50 per cent in 2023 is sought. All African countries except the Central African Republic and Zimbabwe registered progress in reducing their maternal mortality ratio between 2013 and 2015. The increase in the Central African Republic may be attributed to the ongoing conflict in the country, whereas that of Zimbabwe can be attributed to the high HIV/AIDS burden.

Factors influencing the slow progress on the continent include low skilled attendance at delivery, a low prevalence and uptake of modern contraceptives and high unmet needs for family planning, a low met need for emergency obstetric and neonatal care, the persistence of sexual and gender-based violence and high adolescent fertility rates. In the Southern Africa region, HIV/AIDS also remains a major cause of maternal deaths.

In Ethiopia, where the highest percentage decline in the maternal mortality ratio was recorded, some innovative practices are yielding results. These include task-sharing for maternal newborn child and adolescent health and family planning, which is improving critical services to lower levels of care; increased political will through strong collaboration and partnerships between the Government and partners in improving skilled birth attendance by way of the expansion and strengthening of the community health programme, capacity-building of midwives, improved midwifery education and a database for monitoring the midwifery workforce; and reformed laws on abortion and expanded access to safe abortion services. In the United Republic of

Tanzania, the institution of task-sharing mechanisms are ensuring delivery of critical maternal newborn child and adolescent health and family planning services to lower levels of care. Rwanda has also shown that strong political leadership, government ownership and a strong commitment to the maternal newborn child and adolescent health programme improves maternal health. In addition, the institution of a compulsory community-based health insurance scheme as the main source of health financing and performance-based financing, in which community health workers are given basic training in maternal newborn child and adolescent health and given monetary incentives (apart from a basic salary) for improved performance in improving access to reproductive health services at lower levels of care, are having an impact on the maternal mortality situation in the country.

Indicator 3.1.2: proportion of births attended by skilled health personnel

Even though progress was made in the past decade to improve the proportion of births attended by skilled health personnel, giving birth remains risky in Africa (excluding North Africa), compared with the rest of the world. According to data from the Statistics Division, only 51 per cent of births were attended by skilled health personnel in 2015 in Africa (excluding North Africa) (see FIGURE 4.2). Evidence shows that delivery by a skilled birth attendant serves as an indicator of progress towards maternal mortality worldwide, given that it is estimated that between 13 and 33 per cent of maternal deaths could be averted by the presence of such a professional. Eleven African countries, namely, Algeria, Botswana, Cabo Verde, Congo Brazzaville, Egypt, Libya, Mauritius, Sao Tome and Principe, South Africa and Tunisia, reported more than 90 per cent of births being attended by skilled health personnel. Most African countries need to redouble efforts to attain the recommended 90 per cent attendance of births by skilled health workers.

Some of the determining factors for low skilled birth attendance in most African countries include distance from a health facility, financial accessibility and the low educational status of women. Studies have shown that, in Africa, higher per capita incomes and improved maternal education have been associated with improved child and maternal outcomes. Similarly, cost-effective interventions, such as the deployment of

FIGURE 4.1 MATERNAL MORTALITY RATIO BY COUNTRY IN 2013 AND 2015

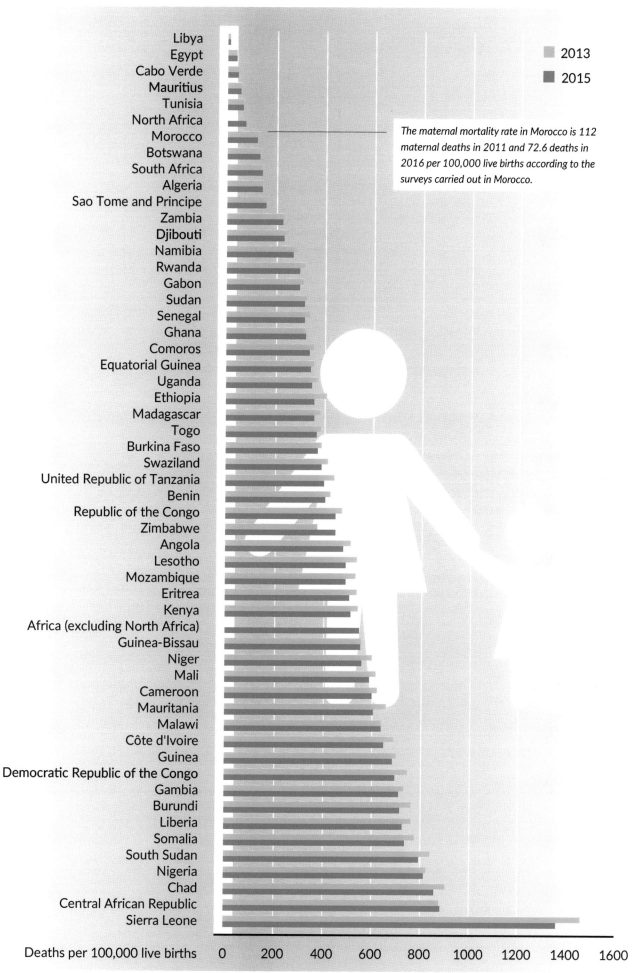

The maternal mortality rate in Morocco is 112 maternal deaths in 2011 and 72.6 deaths in 2016 per 100,000 live births according to the surveys carried out in Morocco.

Deaths per 100,000 live births

Source: Statistics Division (2016).

health extension workers in Ethiopia and community health workers and volunteers in Rwanda to address the immediate and urgent health needs of women in rural areas and at lower levels of care, has gone a long way to improving access to maternal newborn child and adolescent health care (Economic Commission for Africa and Organization for Economic Cooperation and Development, 2014; Basinga et al., 2011). Furthermore, in Rwanda, there was a huge investment in the continuous development and training of a professional health workforce within and outside the country. These programmes, backed by strong leadership, commitment, partnerships and motivation on the part of the health workforce, have succeeded in bringing services closer to the people, in particular rural dwellers, who historically have had challenges in gaining access to health services (World Health Organization, 2013).

Target 3.2 of Sustainable Development Goal 3

By 2030, end preventable deaths of newborns and children under 5 years of age, with all countries aiming to reduce neonatal mortality to at least as low as 12 per 1,000 live births and under-five mortality to at least as low as 25 per 1,000 live births

Related Agenda 2063 targets:

i   Reduce 2013 maternal, neonatal and child mortality rates by at least 50 per cent;

ii Reduce under-five mortality rate attributable to malaria by at least 80 per cent.

The leading causes of death among children between 1 and 59 months of age in Africa are diarrhoea (18 per cent), pneumonia (15 per cent) and malaria (16 per cent). Neonatal deaths account for 29 per cent of under-five mortality, and among newborn babies the main causes include pre-term birth complications, asphyxia and sepsis (African Union, Economic Commission for

FIGURE 4.2 PROPORTION OF BIRTHS ATTENDED BY SKILLED HEALTH PERSONNEL PER REGION

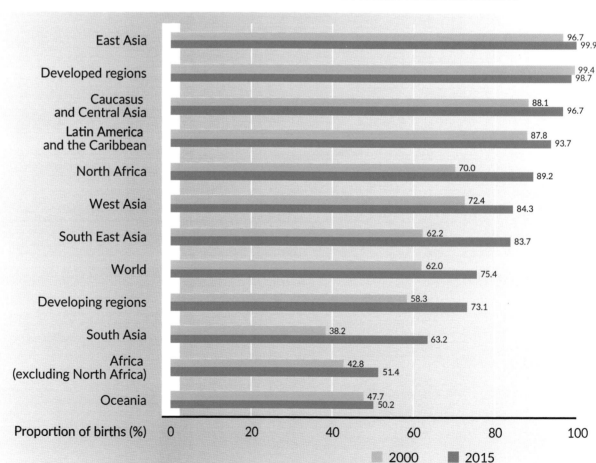

Source: Statistics Division (2016).

FIGURE 4.3 PROPORTION OF BIRTHS ATTENDED BY SKILLED HEALTH PERSONNEL IN AFRICAN COUNTRIES

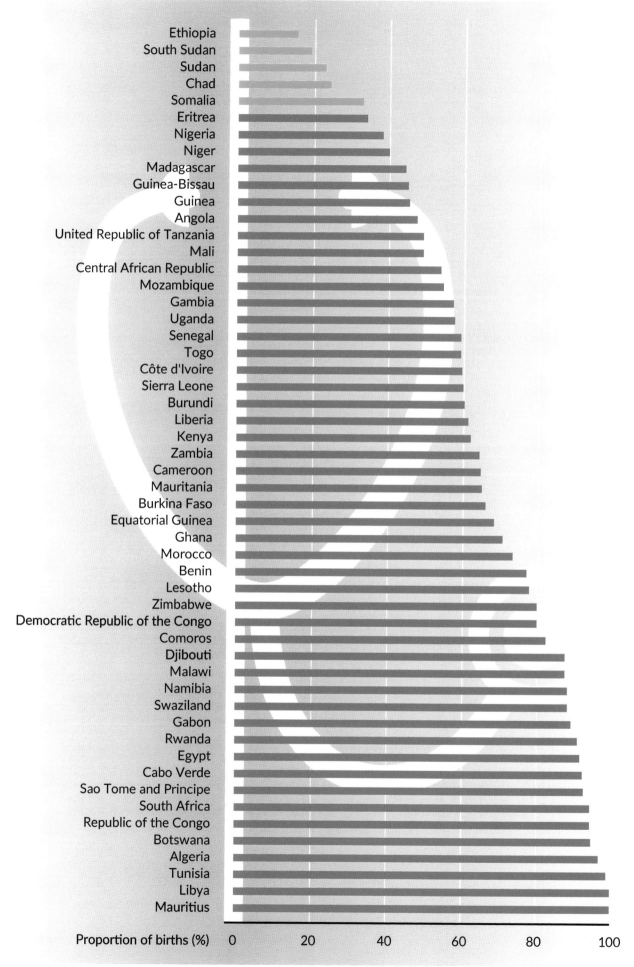

Source: Statistics Division (2016).

FIGURE 4.4 UNDER-FIVE MORTALITY RATE BY REGION

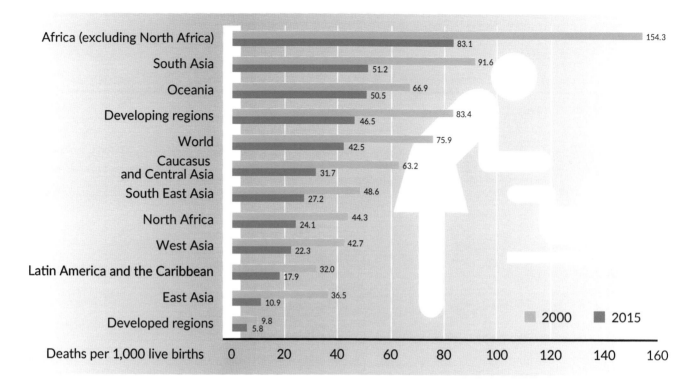

Source: Statistics Division (2016).

Africa, African Development Bank and United Nations Development Programme, 2016). Many African countries have made either slow progress in this regard or experienced stagnating neonatal mortality rates. The situation is worse for the large rural populations of Africa that have poor access to and utilization of maternal and newborn health services.

Improving child survival will depend on the establishment of interventions that will reduce neonatal mortality. Among the proven, cost-effective and high-impact interventions are skilled care at birth and emergency obstetric care; management of pre-term births, including antenatal corticosteroids for lung maturation; basic neonatal care; neonatal resuscitation; early identification and antibiotic treatment of serious infections; inpatient care for small and sick newborns; and prevention of mother-to-child transmission of HIV. Integration of these interventions into the service delivery modalities is also essential. For example, a greater impact will be achieved if quality health services at the health facility are supported by strong outreach, follow-up and referral services. In addition, promoting healthy behaviours at home and making early decisions to seek care will also help to reduce child mortality.[1]

Indicator 3.2.1: under-five mortality rate

The under-five mortality rate is a general indicator of child health and of the socioeconomic, environmental and nutritional status of children. The target is to reduce under-five mortality to at least as low as 25 per 1,000 live births. Agenda 2063 also contains the objective of reducing 2013 levels of under-five mortality by at least 50 per cent in 2023. Since 2000, the global under-five mortality rate has fallen by 44 per cent, from 76 deaths per 1,000 live births in 1990 to 43 deaths per 1,000 live births in 2015. Progress in reducing under-five mortality in Africa (excluding North Africa) has been faster than all other regions of the world: Africa reduced under-five mortality rate by 46 per cent, from 154 deaths per 1,000 live births in 2000 to 83 deaths per 1,000 live births in 2015. However, Africa (excluding North Africa) remains the region with the highest proportion of under-five deaths globally (see FIGURE 4.4).

In 2015, six African countries, namely, Cabo Verde, Egypt, Libya, Mauritius, Seychelles and Tunisia, reported figures below the Sustainable Development Goal target of fewer than 25 deaths per 1,000 live births (see FIGURE 4.5).

---

1   United Nations, (2015)

FIGURE 4.5 UNDER-FIVE MORTALITY RATE BY COUNTRY, 2013 AND 2015

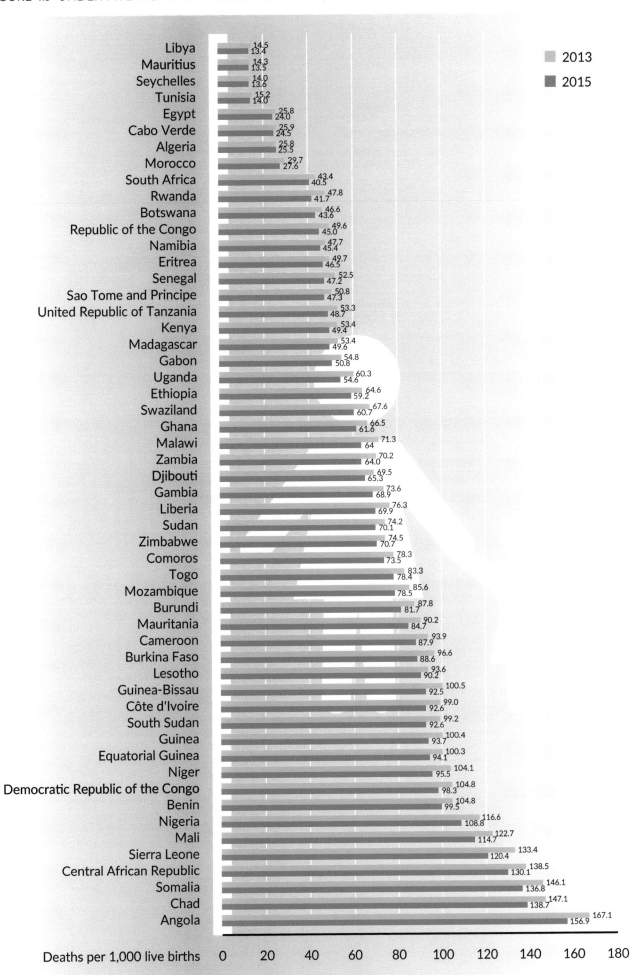

Deaths per 1,000 live births

Source: Statistics Division (2016).

Indicator 3.2.2: neonatal mortality rate

The neonatal mortality rate refers to the number of deaths of newborn babies that occur between birth and the first completed 28 days of life. It is measured as the number of deaths in the first 28 days per 1,000 live births in a given year or period. The majority of child deaths occur during the neonatal period. The rate provides a general measure of the health environment during the earliest stages of life. It is a useful indicator of the quality of care at birth in a country.

Globally, all regions reported an improvement in reducing neonatal mortality between 2000 and 2015. Neonatal mortality in the rest of Africa fell by 30 per cent between 2000 and 2015. However, neonatal mortality remains the highest in the rest of Africa, compared with other regions of the world, except South Asia (see FIGURE 4.6).

In 2015, five African countries, namely, Libya, Mauritius, Seychelles, South Africa and Tunisia, reported figures below the Sustainable Development Goal target of fewer than 12 deaths per 1,000 live births (see FIGURE 4.7).

Target 3.3 of Sustainable Development Goal 3

By 2030, end the epidemics of AIDS, tuberculosis, malaria and neglected tropical diseases and combat hepatitis, water-borne diseases and other communicable diseases

Related Agenda 2063 targets:

i   Reduce the 2013 incidence of HIV/AIDs, malaria and tuberculosis by at least 80 per cent;

ii Reduce the 2013 proportion of deaths attributable to HIV/AIDs, malaria and tuberculosis by at least 50 per cent.

FIGURE 4.6 NEONATAL MORTALITY RATE BY REGION

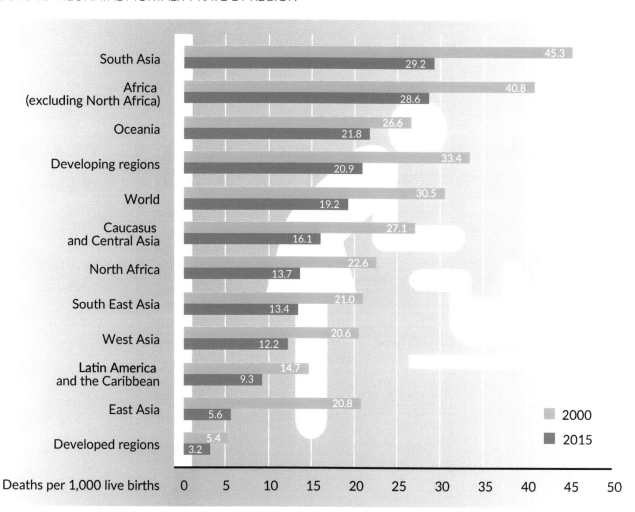

Source: Statistics Division (2016).

FIGURE 4.7 NEONATAL MORTALITY RATE BY COUNTRY

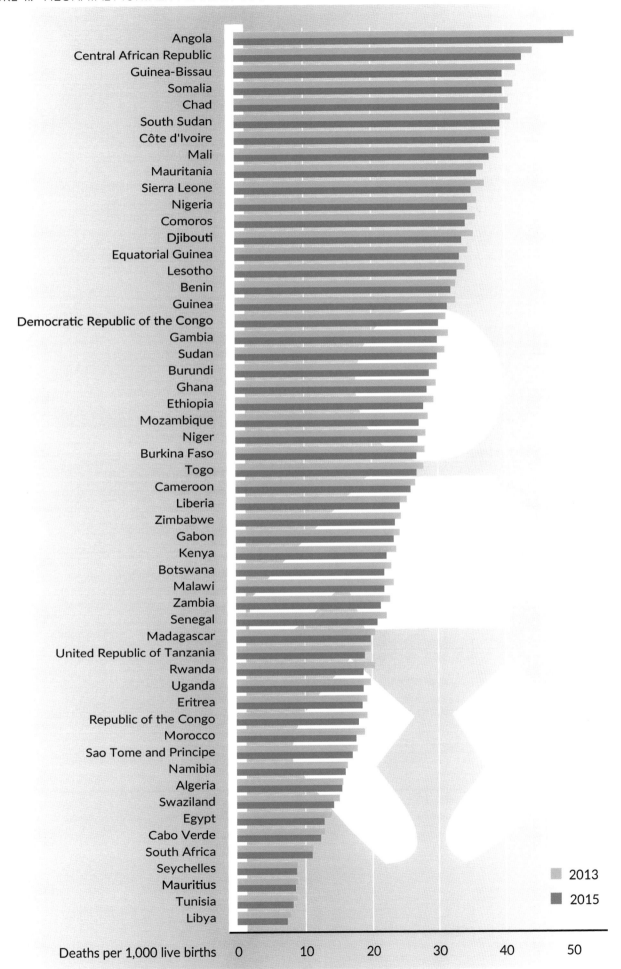

Deaths per 1,000 live births

2013

2015

Source: Statistics Division (2016).

TABLE 4.3 ESTIMATED HIV INCIDENCE RATE BY REGION
(NUMBER OF NEW INFECTIONS PER 1,000 UNINFECTED PEOPLE)

REGION	2000	2005	2010	2015
World	0.55	0.4	0.33	0.3
Developing regions	0.65	0.47	0.37	0.31
North Africa	0.02	0.02	0.02	0.02
Africa (excluding North Africa)	3.87	2.57	1.94	1.48
Latin America and the Caribbean	0.26	0.21	0.18	0.17
East Asia	0.05	0.05	0.04	0.04
South Asia	0.19	0.11	0.08	0.06
South East Asia	0.26	0.27	0.22	0.19
Western Asia	0.01	0.02	0.03	0.04
Oceania	0.76	0.43	0.32	0.33
Caucasus and Central Asia	0.17	0.16	0.1	0.12
Developed regions	0.14	0.15	0.17	0.22

Source: Statistics Division (2016).

TABLE 4.4 ALCOHOL CONSUMPTION BY REGION
(LITRES OF PURE ALCOHOL CONSUMED PER CAPITA)

REGION	2005	2010	2015
World	6	6.2	6.3
Developing regions	4.5	5	5.4
North Africa	0.8	0.7	0.5
Africa (excluding North Africa)	6.2	6.1	6.3
Latin America and the Caribbean	8.4	7.7	7.5
East Asia	5.1	6.8	7.7
South Asia	2.8	3.3	3.8
South East Asia	2.9	3.3	3.8
Western Asia	1.8	1.3	1.5
Oceania	3.2	2.9	3
Caucasus and Central Asia	5.8	5.6	5
Developed regions	11.6	10.8	10.4

Source: Statistics Division (2016).

FIGURE 4.8 ESTIMATED HIV INCIDENCE RATE BY GENDER, 2015

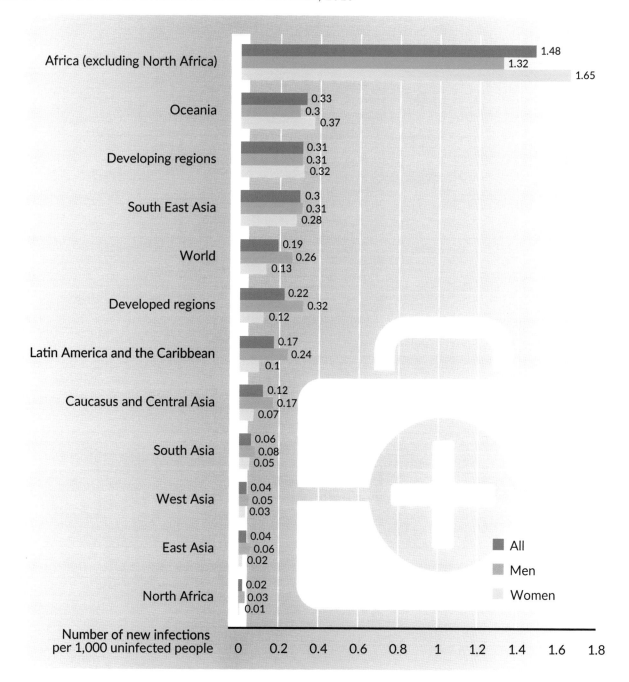

Source: Statistics Division (2016).

Indicator 3.3.1: number of new HIV infections per 1,000 uninfected population by sex, age and key populations

The world has committed itself to ending the AIDS epidemic by 2030. According to the Joint United Nations Programme on HIV/AIDS, the gains in treatment are largely responsible for a 26 per cent decline in AIDS-related deaths globally since 2010, from an estimated 1.5 million in 2010 to 1.1 million in 2015. HIV infections globally were 0.3 per 1,000 uninfected people, and an estimated 2.1 million people became newly infected in 2015. The incidence of HIV was highest in Africa (excluding North Africa), with 1.5 new cases per 1,000 uninfected people in 2015 (see TABLE 4.3).

In the rest of Africa, Oceania and the developing regions as a whole, the HIV incidence among women was more prevalent than among men in 2015 (see FIGURE 4.8).

Target 3.4 of Sustainable Development Goal 3

By 2030, reduce by one third premature mortality from non-communicable diseases through prevention and treatment and promote health and well-being

There are no data to describe the status with regard to achieving this target.

Target 3.5 of Sustainable Development Goal 3

Strengthen the prevention and treatment of substance abuse, including narcotic drug abuse and harmful use of alcohol

Agenda 2063 has no related targets.

Indicator 3.5.2: harmful use of alcohol, defined according to the national context as alcohol per capita consumption (15 years of age and older) within a calendar year in litres of pure alcohol

The harmful use of alcohol is a serious health burden and affects everyone. Health problems from dangerous alcohol use arise in the form of acute and chronic conditions, and adverse social consequences are common when they are associated with alcohol consumption (World Health Organization, 2010). Globally, average alcohol consumption was reported at 6.3 litres of pure alcohol per capita among those 15 years of age and older. In 2015, alcohol consumption was the highest in developed regions and the lowest in North Africa. The consumption of alcohol increased globally (see TABLE 4.4).

Target 3.6 of Sustainable Development Goal 3

By 2020, halve the number of global death and injuries from road traffic accidents

Agenda 2063 has no related targets.

Indicator 3.6.1: death rate due to road traffic injuries

At the global level, the rest of Africa is the region with the highest rate of death and injuries from road traffic accidents, notwithstanding a declining trend (see FIGURE 4.9).

FIGURE 4.9 DEATH RATE DUE TO ROAD TRAFFIC INJURIES

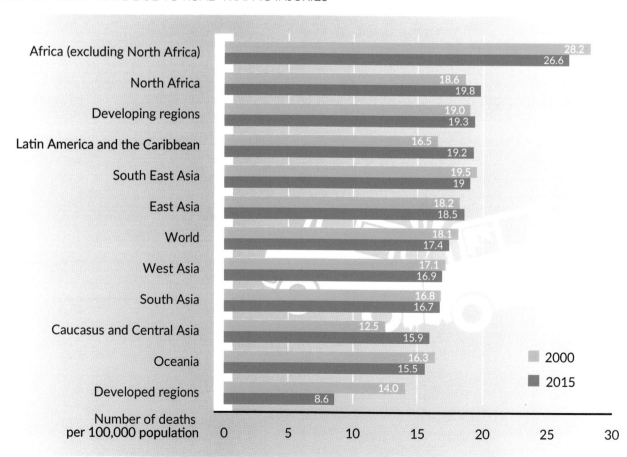

Source: Statistics Division (2016).

Target 3.7 of Sustainable Development Goal 3

By 2030, ensure universal access to sexual and reproductive health-care services, including for family planning, information and education, and the integration of reproductive health into national strategies and programmes

Related Agenda 2063 target:

i   Increase 2013 levels of access to sexual and reproductive health services to women by at least 30 per cent.

Indicator 3.7.1: proportion of women married or in a union of reproductive age (between 15 and 49 years) who have their need for family planning satisfied with modern methods

Globally, the proportion of women who are married or in a union who have their need for family planning satisfied with modern methods improved between 2000 and 2015 in all regions, except East Asia, which

saw a slight decline. In 2015, Africa (excluding North Africa), however, had the lowest (less than 50 per cent) proportion of women who are married or in a union and had their need for family planning satisfied with modern methods (see FIGURE 4.10).

Governments must make strong efforts to invest in family planning and other reproductive health services going forward, given that they are cost-effective, save lives and are cornerstones of sustainable development.

FIGURE 4.10 MARRIED WOMEN OR THOSE IN A UNION OF REPRODUCTIVE AGE (BETWEEN 15 AND 49 YEARS) WHO HAVE THEIR NEED FOR FAMILY PLANNING SATISFIED WITH MODERN METHODS, BY REGION

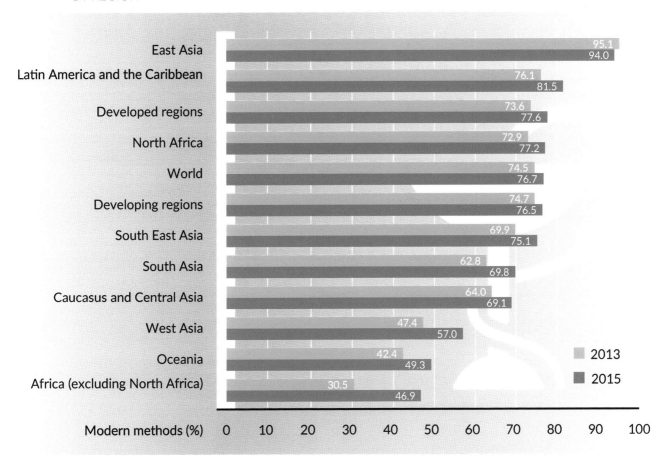

Source: Statistics Division (2016).

If all unmet needs for family planning were satisfied, unintended pregnancies would drop by 83 per cent, from 18 million to 3 million annually, and unsafe abortions would decline by 84 per cent, from 5.7 million to 0.9 million (Singh et al., 2014). If the full provision of modern contraception were combined with integrated and improved care, including HIV-related services for all pregnant women and newborns, maternal deaths would drop by 69 per cent, from 183,000 to 58,000 annually; newborn deaths would drop by 82 per cent, from 1.2 million to 213,000; and HIV infections among newborns would decline by 93 per cent, from 115,000 to 8,000. Other long-term gains from meeting women's sexual and reproductive health needs include improvements in women's educational attainment, labour force participation, productivity and earnings, as well as higher household savings and assets. Governments must make strong efforts to invest in family planning and other reproductive health services going forward, given that they are cost-effective, save lives and are cornerstones of sustainable development.

Indicator 3.7.2: adolescent birth rate per 1,000 adolescent women between 15 and 19 years of age

Almost all regions, except South East Asia, saw a decline in adolescent birth rates among girls between 15 and 19 years of age during the period 2000-2015. Although the rest of Africa made progress in reducing the adolescent birth rate by 21 per cent between 2000 and 2015, in 2015 it remained the region in the world with the highest adolescent birth rate, at 102 births per 1,000 women between 15 and 19 years of age (see FIGURE 4.11). Twenty-five African countries have adolescent birth rates of more than 100 births per 1,000 women aged between 15 and 19 years. Only nine African countries have reported adolescent birth rates of fewer than 50 births per 1,000 women between 15 and 19 years of age.

The consequences of adolescent pregnancy on mother and child are serious. These include unsafe abortions and its associated consequences, anaemia, malaria, HIV

FIGURE 4.11 ADOLESCENT BIRTH RATE AMONG WOMEN AGED 15 AND 19 YEARS BY REGION, 2000 AND 2015

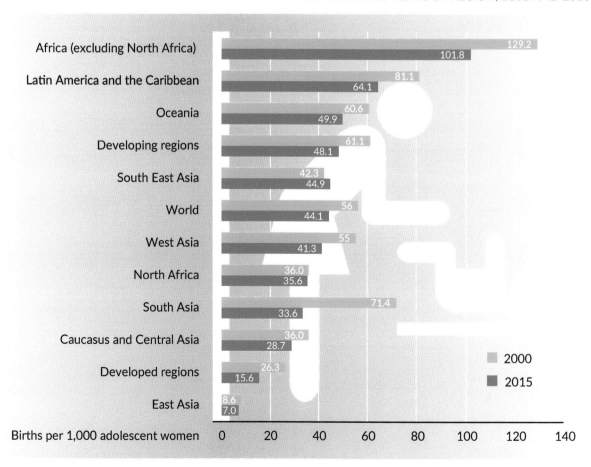

Source: Statistics Division (2016).

and other sexually transmitted infections, postpartum haemorrhage, mental disorders such as depression, and obstetric fistula.[2]

The rates of pre-term birth, low birth weight and asphyxia are higher among the children of adolescents, all of which increase the chance of death and future health problems for the baby. Given that the majority (66 per cent) of African countries still have high adolescent births, the implications for mother and child have far-reaching consequences for socioeconomic development.

There is therefore a need to scale up essential interventions that are critical to improving reproductive health and reducing maternal and child death. There is also a need to scale up partnerships with all stakeholders.

4.4 Conclusion

The review of the progress made in achieving Sustainable Development Goal 3, which is aligned with goal 3 of Agenda 2063, has placed an emphasis on significant gains in health during the past decade, including a considerable decline in child and maternal mortality. Nevertheless, the continent remains the region with the highest burden of maternal and child deaths, compared with other regions around the world. Progress also remains varied between and among subregions and individual countries.

Low and inequitable access to skilled health personnel at birth, the high adolescent birth rate and access to family planning remain challenges to addressing maternal health in Africa. A lack of data, especially disaggregated data, also remains a challenge for proper monitoring and evaluation.

There is therefore a need to scale up essential interventions that are critical to improving reproductive health and reducing maternal and child deaths. There is also a need to scale up partnerships with all stakeholders to complete the unfinished business of the Millennium Development Goals and effectively implement Agenda 2063 and the 2030 Agenda in an integrated manner.

Strong and robust monitoring and evaluation frameworks should be put in place to inform analysis and policy design and implementation. Building the capacity of national statistical offices is therefore critical to responding to the huge data demand. Strengthening civil registration systems will also facilitate tracking the progress of Sustainable Development Goal

... the continent remains the region with the highest burden of maternal and child deaths, compared with other regions around the world. Progress also remains varied between and among subregions and individual countries.

2   WHO, (2006) http://apps.who.int/iris/bitst ream/10665/43368/1/9241593784_eng.pdf

CHAPTER 5

Sustainable Development Goal 5: Gender equality

5.1 Introduction

Sustainable Development Goal 5, to achieve gender equality and empower all women and girls, underscores the importance of improving gender equality and opportunities for sustainable development and how the negative impact of discrimination against women and girls can impede economic and social development. Gender equality is integral to sustainable development and an essential ingredient for economic progress. When women and girls have the means to fully participate in and contribute to socioeconomic development, direct and indirect benefits lead to the betterment of societies and nation States as a whole.

> **Gender equality is integral to sustainable development and an essential ingredient for economic progress.**

Although much progress has been made in achieving gender equality in Africa, progress has been slow and varied across the region. Compared with the previous decades, gender disparities between men and women have narrowed. Girls are now enrolling in school in higher numbers than ever before and gender gaps in school enrolment at the primary and secondary level are closing. Women now have better access to health care than in previous decades, leading to better health outcomes. Owing to improvements in women's reproductive rights and reproductive health care, maternal mortality ratios in most countries in Africa have decreased. As greater numbers of women are seeking employment in the formal and the informal sector, the gender disparity in labour force participation has reduced. Compared with other regions, the gap in labour force participation is smaller in Africa.

However, several challenges remain in various spheres and across multiple levels. Social mores and traditions continue to pose major obstacles to women's empowerment, and structural constraints further undermine progress. Traditional gender roles dictate that women carry a heavier burden of work and have poorer access to resources and opportunities, compared with men. Women continue to be victims of various forms of violence, both in the household and in public spaces. Violence against women can be especially severe in conflict-affected settings and during periods of war. Women in the region experience worse health outcomes than women in other regions. Africa continues to experience the highest burden of maternal deaths in relation to other regions of the world. At the structural level, weak infrastructure, law enforcement and poor quality of public services pose major obstacles to women's empowerment and progress on gender equality.

5.2 Targets and alignment with Agenda 2063

Sustainable Development Goal 5 has 9 targets with 14 indicators and is aligned with goals 3, 5, 10 and 17, the latter of which is full gender equality in all spheres of life, of Agenda 2063 (see TABLE 5.1).

TARGETS OF SUSTAINABLE DEVELOPMENT GOAL 5	TARGETS OF GOALS 3, 5, 10 AND 17 OF AGENDA 2063*
5.1 End all forms of discrimination against all women and girls everywhere	**6.17.2.2** Reduce by 50 per cent all harmful social norms and customary practices against women and girls and those that promote violence and discrimination against women and girls
	6.17.2.4 End all forms of political, legal or administrative discrimination against women and girls by 2023
	6.17.1.1 Equal economic rights for women, including the rights to own and inherit property, sign a contract, save, register and manage a business and own and operate a bank account by 2026
	6.17.2.1 Reduce 2013 levels of violence against women and girls by at least 20%
5.2 Eliminate all forms of violence against all women and girls in the public and private spheres, including trafficking and sexual and other types of exploitation	**6.17.2.1** Reduce 2013 levels of violence against women and girls by at least 20%
5.3 Eliminate all harmful practices, such as child, early and forced marriage and female genital mutilation	**6.17.2.2** Reduce by 50 per cent all harmful social norms and customary practices against women and girls and those that promote violence and discrimination against women and girls
5.4 Recognize and value unpaid care and domestic work through the provision of public services, infrastructure and social protection policies and the promotion of shared responsibility within the household and the family as nationally appropriate	**6.17.1.2** At least 20 per cent of women in rural areas have access to and control productive assets, including land and grants, credit, inputs, financial services and information
5.5 Ensure women's full and effective participation and equal opportunities for leadership at all levels of decision-making in political, economic and public life	**6.17.1.1** Equal economic rights for women, including the rights to own and inherit property, sign a contract, save, register and manage a business and own and operate a bank account by 2026
	6.17.1.2 At least 20 per cent of women in rural areas have access to and control productive assets, including land and grants, credit, inputs, financial services and information
	6.17.1.3 At least 30 per cent of all elected officials at local, regional and national levels and in judicial institutions are women
	6.17.1.5 Increase gender parity in decision-making positions at all levels to at least 50-50 between women and men
5.6 Ensure universal access to sexual and reproductive health and reproductive rights as agreed in accordance with the Programme of Action of the International Conference on Population and Development and the Beijing Platform for Action and the outcome documents of their review conferences	**1.3.1.2** Increase 2013 levels of access to sexual and reproductive health services to women by at least 30 per cent

CHAPTER 5   SUSTAINABLE DEVELOPMENT GOAL 5: GENDER EQUALITY

TABLE 5.1 (CONT)

TARGETS OF SUSTAINABLE DEVELOPMENT GOAL 5	TARGETS OF GOALS 3, 5, 10 AND 17 OF AGENDA 2063*
	1.5.1.3 Increase participation of young people and women in integrated agricultural value chains by at least 30 per cent
	1.5.1.3 Increase participation of young people and women in integrated agricultural value chains by at least 30 per cent
5.a Undertake reforms to give women equal rights to economic resources, as well as access to ownership and control over land and other forms of property, financial services, inheritance and natural resources, in accordance with national laws	**6.17.1.1** Equal economic rights for women, including the rights to own and inherit property, sign a contract, save, register and manage a business and own and operate a bank account by 2026
	6.17.1.2 At least 20 per cent of women in rural areas have access to and control productive assets, including land and grants, credit, inputs, financial services and information
	6.17.1.4 At least 25 per cent of annual public procurement at national and subnational levels are awarded to women
	2.10.1.5 Double information and communications technology penetration and contribution to GDP
	2.10.1.6 Realize at least a 70 per cent increase in broadband accessibility by 2020
5.b Enhance the use of enabling technology, in particular information and communications technology, to promote the empowerment of women	**2.10.1.7** Digital broadcasting is achieved as the norm by 2016
	2.10.1.5 Double information and communications technology penetration and contribution to GDP
	2.10.1.8 Attain 100 per cent mobile penetration by 2020
	6.17.1.3 At least 30 per cent of all elected officials at local, regional and national levels and in judicial institutions are women
5.c Adopt and strengthen sound policies and enforceable legislation for the promotion of gender equality and the empowerment of all women and girls at all levels	**6.17.1.4** At least 25 per cent of annual public procurement at national and subnational levels are awarded to women
	6.17.1.6 Solemn declaration index developed by the "Gender is my agenda" campaign and ECA on gender is computed biannually and used in making policy/resource allocation decisions
	6.17.2.4 End all forms of political, legal or administrative discrimination against women and girls by 2023

Source: Authors' own analysis based on Statistics Division (2017b) and African Union Commission (2015).

* *Goal 3 (healthy and well-nourished citizens) and goal 5 (modern agriculture for increased productivity and production) of aspiration 1; goal 10 (world-class infrastructure criss-crosses Africa) of aspiration 2; and goal 17 (full gender equality in all spheres or life) of aspiration 6.*

5.3 Synergies between the 2030 Agenda, Agenda 2063 and the Beijing Declaration and Platform for Action

Both the 2030 Agenda and Agenda 2063 are aimed at furthering the progress made on gender equality in a sustainable and equitable manner. Sustainable Development Goal 5 concerns achieving gender equality and the empowerment of all women and girls, while goal 17 of Agenda 2063 is aimed at achieving full gender equality in all spheres of life. The two agendas consider gender equality to be a development goal in its own right. In addition, they contain reaffirmations of the centrality of gender equality to the realization of structural transformation of African economies towards an equitable and sustainable development on the continent and are consistent with prior international commitments, including the Beijing Declaration and Platform for Action, which envisaged a world in which each woman and girl can exercise her freedoms and choices and realize all her rights, including the right to live free from violence, to go to school, to participate in decisions and to earn equal pay for equal work. The 12 areas of concern of the Beijing Platform for Action are consistent with the priority areas of Sustainable Development Goal 5 and goal 17 of Agenda 2063, and they are mutually reinforcing. Such dynamic consistency will make it easy to harness and support countries' efforts to fully implement both goals in terms of achieving gender equality and women/girls' empowerment on the continent. FIGURE 5.1 outlines the synergies between the Beijing Declaration and Platform for Action, Agenda 2063 and the 2030 Agenda.

FIGURE 5.1 SYNERGIES BETWEEN THE BEIJING DECLARATION AND PLATFORM FOR ACTION, AGENDA 2063 AND THE 2030 AGENDA

Beijing Platform for Action

- Accelerate gender equality and the advancement of all women
- Twelve areas of concern:
  · Women and poverty;
  · Education and training;
  · Women and health;
  · Violence against women;
  · Women and armed conflict;

· Women and the economy;
· Women in power and decision-making;
· Institutional mechanisms for the advancement of women;
· Human rights of women;
· Women and the media;
· Women and the environment;
· The girl child.

Agenda 2063

- Goal 17: Achieve full gender equality in all spheres of life

· Priority areas:
  · Women's empowerment;
  · Violence and discrimination against women and girls.

2030 Agenda

- Goal 5: Achieve gender equality
- and empower all women and girls
- Priority areas:
  · Discrimination against women and girls;
  · Violence against women;
  · Harmful practices such as child early and forced marriage and female genital mutilation;

· Unpaid care and domestic work;
· Women's equal rights to economic resources;
· Use of technology;
· Policies and enforceable legislation for the promotion of gender equality and the empowerment of all women and girls.

5.4 Current status and progress

Monitoring progress on Sustainable Development Goal 5, which is aimed at achieving gender equality and empowering all women and girls, will be especially critical in Africa. Currently, however, there is limited availability of data on gender indicators for each of the targets of Goal 5. The analytical scope of the chapter was limited owing to data constraints. When possible, data from the United Nations Sustainable Development Goal portal were used for the analysis, and, in other instances, data from the World Bank's World Development Indicators portal were used.

Target 5.1 of Sustainable Development Goal 5
End all forms of discrimination against all women and girls everywhere

Related Agenda 2063 targets:

i   Reduce by 50 per cent all harmful social norms and customary practices against women and girls and those that promote violence and discrimination against women and girls;

ii   End all forms of political, legal or administrative discrimination against women and girls by 2023;

iii   Equal economic rights for women, including the rights to own and inherit property, sign a contract, save, register and manage a business and own and operate a bank account by 2026;

iv   Reduce 2013 levels of violence against women and girls by at least 20 per cent.

Indicator 5.1.1: whether legal frameworks are in place to promote, enforce and monitor equality and non-discrimination on the basis of sex

A review of African legal frameworks suggests that, while progress has been made, a number of countries still have laws that discriminate against women in the private and public spheres. An index was constructed to measure the extent to which countries had adopted gender-equal laws. The index measured whether a country had laws on equal remuneration, non-discrimination in hiring, paid or unpaid maternity leave, domestic violence, criminalized marital rape and sexual harassment. A score of six indicated that a country had adopted all six laws and zero if it had none.

FIGURE 5.2   ADOPTION OF GENDER-EQUAL LAWS BY AFRICAN (EXCLUDING NORTH AFRICAN) COUNTRIES BY SCORE ON LEGAL INDEX

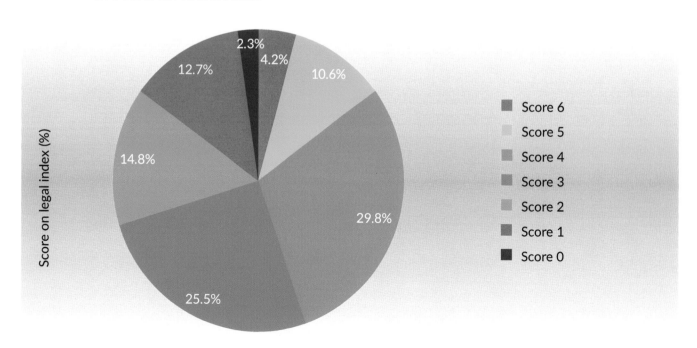

Source: World Bank.

...while progress has been made, a number of countries still have laws that discriminate against women in the private and public spheres.

Data from Africa (excluding North Africa) show that, of 47 countries, 4.2 per cent had adopted all six gender egalitarian laws (see FIGURE 5.2). The majority of the countries (29.8 per cent) had adopted four of the six laws and 25.5 per cent had adopted three of six. The findings indicate that most countries have adopted at least one or more gender-equal laws that protect women's rights to some extent. However, full legal protection, as would have been captured by a maximum score on the legal index, has not been attained except in two countries. Only Namibia and Zimbabwe have adopted all six gender egalitarian laws.

Target 5.2 of Sustainable Development Goal 5:
eliminate all forms of violence against all women and girls

Related Agenda 2063 target:

i   Reduce 2013 levels of violence against women and girls by at least 20 per cent.

Indicator 5.2.1: proportion of ever-partnered women and girls 15 years of age and older subjected to physical,

FIGURE 5.3 WOMEN SUBJECTED TO PHYSICAL/SEXUAL VIOLENCE IN SELECTED COUNTRIES

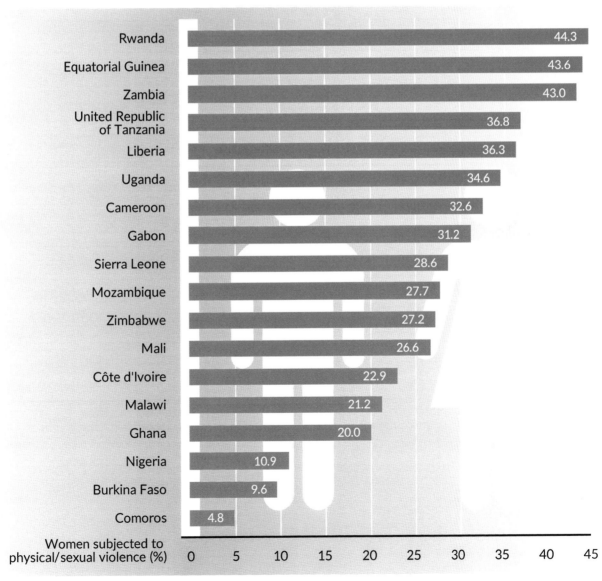

Rwanda	44.3
Equatorial Guinea	43.6
Zambia	43.0
United Republic of Tanzania	36.8
Liberia	36.3
Uganda	34.6
Cameroon	32.6
Gabon	31.2
Sierra Leone	28.6
Mozambique	27.7
Zimbabwe	27.2
Mali	26.6
Côte d'Ivoire	22.9
Malawi	21.2
Ghana	20.0
Nigeria	10.9
Burkina Faso	9.6
Comoros	4.8

Women subjected to physical/sexual violence (%)   0   5   10   15   20   25   30   35   40   45

Source: UN Statistics Division.

sexual or psychological violence by a current or former intimate partner in the previous 12 months, by form of violence and by age

Data from selected countries in Africa (except North Africa) indicate a high prevalence of violence against women. In a large number of countries, more than one third of women had reported being subjected to physical or sexual violence (see FIGURE 5.3). The rates were as high as 43 to 44 per cent in some countries. In some Fragile States, sexual violence against women has been used as a weapon of war. Violence against women not only has a debilitating psychological impact on its victims and future generations, but also has also been found to be associated with poor health outcomes during pregnancy and a higher risk of acquiring diseases such as HIV. While several countries have adopted gender-based violence laws in the region, there remain significant gaps in reporting

The practice of child marriage not only negates opportunities for education and self-advancement for women, but also puts their health and survival prospects at risk.

violence and law enforcement. Owing to the stigma and notions of shame associated with violence, victims tend not to report it and fail to seek justice. Weak and insensitive law enforcement further deters victims of violence from coming forward and seeking appropriate redressal.

Target 5.3 of Sustainable Development Goal 5:
elimination of all harmful practices, such as child, early and forced marriage and female genital mutilation

Related Agenda 2063 target:

i   Reduce by 50 per cent all harmful social norms and customary practices against women and girls and those that promote violence and discrimination against women and girls.

Studies of the Democratic Republic of the Congo and Uganda show that child marriages are associated with lower education levels, lower wealth and higher labour force participation rates.

Indicator 5.3.1: proportion of women between 20 and 24 years of age who were married or in a union before age 15 and before 18 years of age

Child marriages have a debilitating impact on growth and the development prospects of young girls, undermining their ability to realize their optimal potential. In most countries of the region, customs and traditions dictate that girls marry and begin childbearing early. The practice of child marriage not only negates opportunities for education and self-advancement for women, but also puts their health and survival prospects at risk.

Studies in the Democratic Republic of the Congo and Uganda show that child marriages are associated with lower education levels, lower wealth and higher labour force participation rates (Male and Wodon, 2016a; 2016b). Early childbearing is associated with higher levels of fertility and a higher risk of maternal mortality. Trends show that some countries in Africa have attained greater success than others in delaying the age of marriage among women. Less than 10 per cent of women between 20 and 24 years of age were married by 18 years of age in countries such as Djibouti, Rwanda, Swaziland and Tunisia (see FIGURE 5.4). At the other end of the spectrum, the highest prevalence of child marriages was observed in the Central African Republic, Guinea, Niger and South Sudan. In these countries, more than 50 per cent of women between 20 and 24 years of age were married by 18 years of age. In Niger, where the highest prevalence of child marriages exists, more than 75 per cent of women between the ages of 20 and 24 were married before reaching 18 years of age.

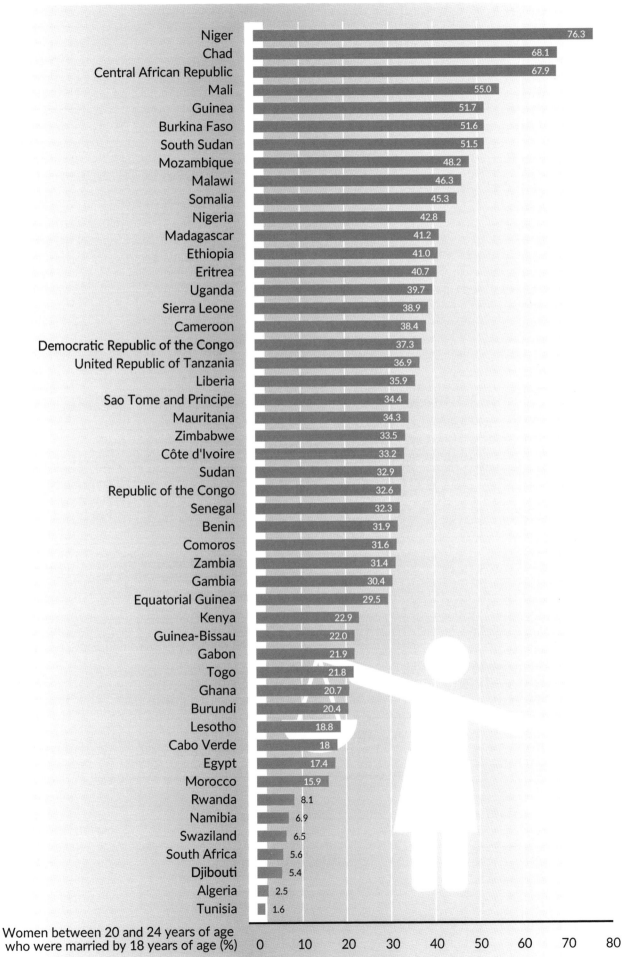

Women between 20 and 24 years of age who were married by 18 years of age (%)

Source: Statistics Division (2017).

FIGURE 5.5 EARLY MARRIAGE IN AFRICA

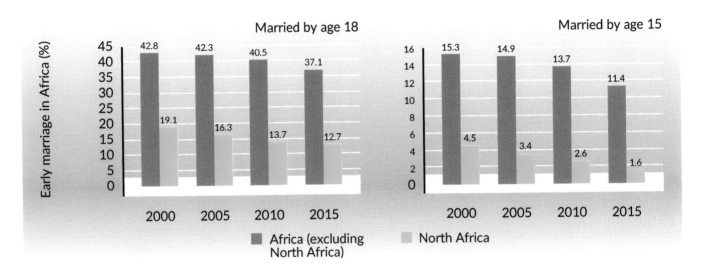

Source: Statistics Division (2017).

FIGURE 5.6 PROPORTION OF GIRLS BETWEEN THE 15 AND 19 YEARS OF AGE WHO HAVE UNDERGONE FEMALE GENITAL MUTILATION/CIRCUMCISION

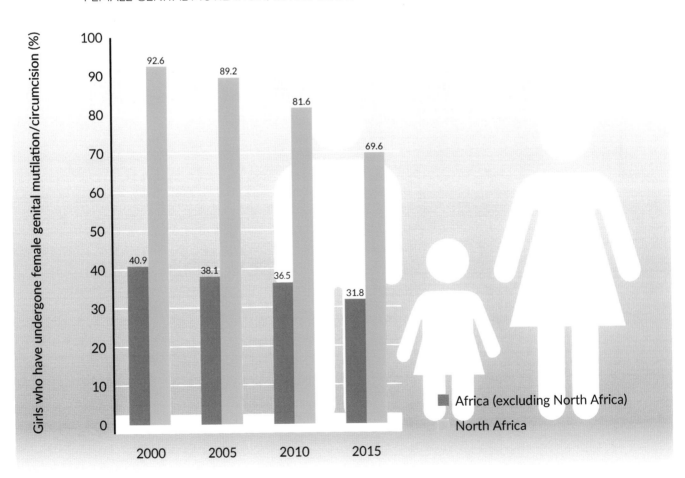

Source: Statistics Division (2017).

Overall, the prevalence of child marriage has shown declining trends in the region, both in North Africa and the rest of Africa (see FIGURE 5.5-A). A subregional comparison of the child marriage data further shows that the practice is far more prevalent in Africa (excluding North Africa). Child marriage by 15 years of age is more prevalent in Africa (excluding North Africa) than in North Africa (see FIGURE 5.5-B). Trends show that the pace of decline of child marriage has been moderate in both subregions. In Africa (excluding North Africa), the proportion of women between 20 and 24 years of age who married by 18 years of age declined from 43 per cent in 2000 to 37 per cent in 2015; and in North Africa, the proportion declined from 19 to 13 per cent during the same period.

Indicator 5.3.2: proportion of girls and women between 15 and 49 years of age who have undergone female genital mutilation/cutting, by age

Millions of young girls have been subjected to the barbaric practice of female genital mutilation or cutting as a means of curbing their sexual behaviour as they transition into adolescence. The practice of female genital mutilation, although widely acknowledged as a human right violation, remains highly prevalent in the region. According to the World Health Organization (2017), female genital mutilation reflects deep-rooted inequality between the sexes and constitutes an extreme form of discrimination against women. While the exact number of girls and women globally who have undergone the procedure is unknown, it is estimated that at least 200 million have been subjected to the procedure in 30 countries (United Nations, 2016b). In 2015, almost 70 per cent of girls between 15 and 19 years of age had undergone female genital mutilation in North Africa, down from more than 90 per cent in 2000 (see FIGURE 5.6). The prevalence in the rest of Africa is also high but relatively lower, compared with North Africa, with about 32 percent of girls having suffered mutilation in 2015. The harmful practice has shown declining trends during the past 15 years and the pace of decline is greater in the North Africa subregion, compared with the rest of Africa.

Target 5.5 of Sustainable Development Goal 5:

Ensure women's full and effective participation and equal opportunities for leadership at all levels of decision-making in political, economic and public life

Related Agenda 2063 target:

i   Equal economic rights for women, including the rights to own and inherit property, sign a contract, save, register and manage a business and own and operate a bank account by 2026;

ii At least 20 per cent of women in rural areas have access to and control productive assets, including land and grants, credit, inputs, financial service and information;

iii At least 30 per cent of all elected officials at the local, regional and national levels are women, as well as in judicial institutions;

iv Increase gender parity in decision-making positions at all levels to at least 50-50 between women and men.

Indicator 5.5.1: proportion of seats held by women in national parliaments and local governments

Women continue to be underrepresented in the political sphere, but encouraging progress was evident with regard to increasing women's representation in national parliaments.

Women continue to be underrepresented in the political sphere, but encouraging progress was evident with regard to increasing women's representation in national parliaments. The proportion of women in national parliaments increased significantly in both subregions. In Africa (excluding North Africa), the proportion of seats held by women in national parliaments increased from 10.2 per cent in 1997 to 23.5 per cent in 2016 (see FIGURE 5.7). Africa (excluding North Africa) reported higher representation of women in parliaments, compared with North Africa, in 2000. However, tremendous progress was seen in North Africa during the subsequent 16 years. From 2000 to 2016, the proportion of women in national parliaments quadru-

FIGURE 5.7 PROPORTION OF WOMEN IN NATIONAL PARLIAMENTS, 2016

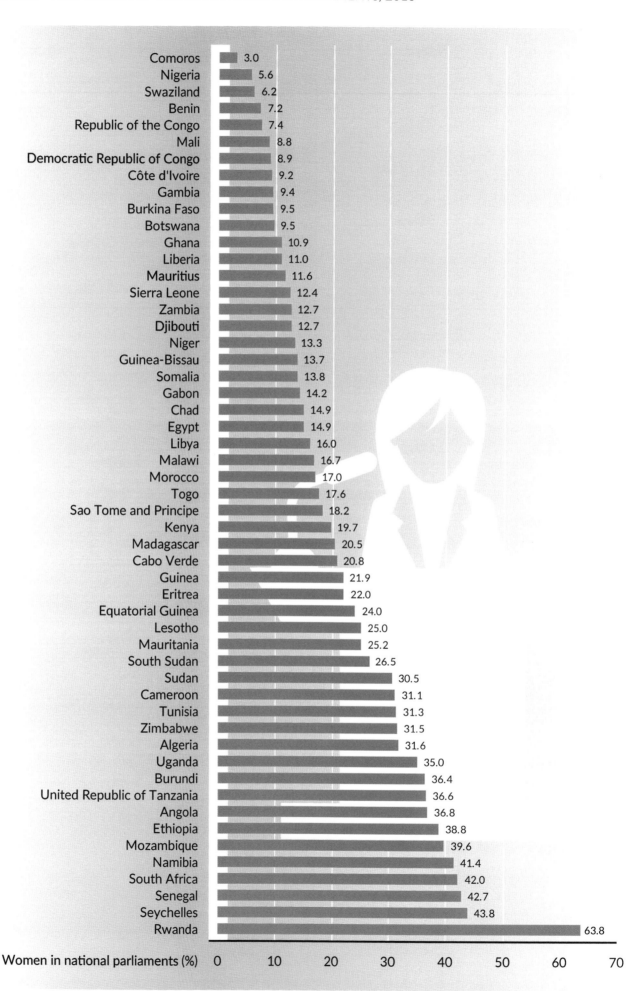

Women in national parliaments (%)

FIGURE 5.8 PROPORTION PEOPLE WITH AN ACCOUNT AT A FINANCIAL INSTITUTION IN AFRICA (EXCLUDING NORTH AFRICA)

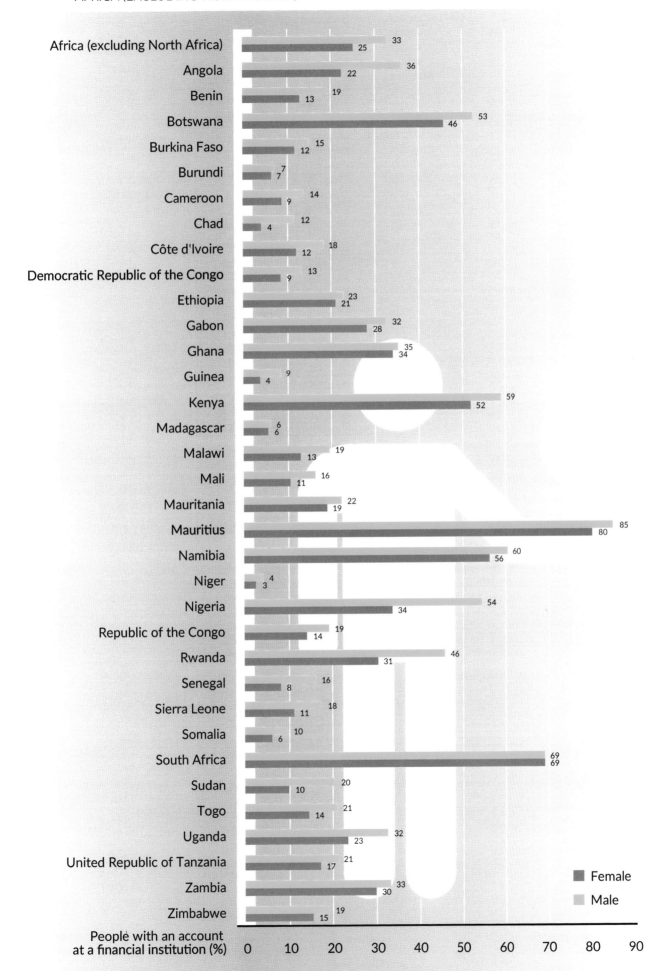

Source: World Bank.

pled in North Africa and, by 2016, the gap between the two subregions had substantially closed.

Some countries in the region have demonstrated exemplary progress in increasing women's representation in national parliaments (see FIGURE 5.7). Rwanda, a country where women hold nearly 64 per cent of seats in the national parliament, ranks as the highest level of women's representation in parliament in the world.

Access to a financial institution tends to be lower among women compared with men.

Countries such as Namibia, Senegal and South Africa also report high rates of representation of women's political participation, ranging between 41 to 44 per cent of seats in national parliaments. Furthermore, countries such as Liberia, Malawi and Mozambique have had women leaders as heads of State and several other countries have had female Vice-Presidents.

Notwithstanding the successes observed in selected countries, women's political leadership remains below par in most countries of the region. The vast majority of countries do not have equal representation of men and women in national parliaments. The lack of women's representation in policymaking and governance has

implications for the advancement of gender equality in countries. Research shows that women in politics raise issues that others overlook, pass bills that others oppose, invest in projects others dismiss, seek to end abuses that others ignore and are more likely to reach peace agreements (National Democratic Institute, 2017).

Target 5.a of Sustainable Development Goal 5

Undertake reforms to give women equal rights to economic resources and access to ownership and control over land and other forms of property, financial services, inheritance and natural resources, in accordance with national laws

Access to a financial institution tends to be lower among women compared with men. Low levels of access to finances limits women's access to resources and their opportunities for economic empowerment. In most countries in the region, data show a lower percentage of women have an account at a financial institution, compared with men (see FIGURE 5.8). The data captured whether men and women respondents 15 years of age and older reported having an account by themselves or someone else at a bank or another financial institution. With the exception of South Africa, access to a financial institution was consistently lower among women compared with men. On average, 25.1 per cent of women in Africa (excluding North Africa) have access to a financial institution, compared with 32.7 per cent of men.

FIGURE 5.9   MOBILE ACCOUNT OWNERSHIP IN AFRICA (EXCLUDING NORTH AFRICA)

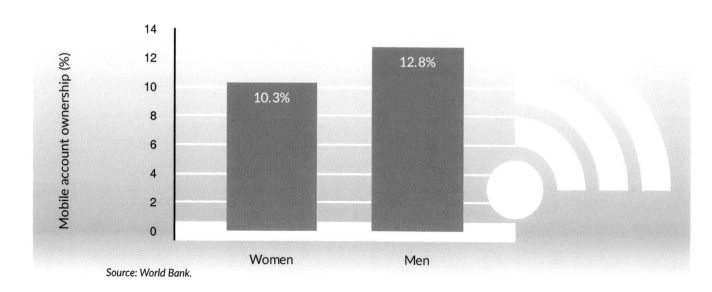

Source: World Bank.

Target 5.b of Sustainable Development Goal 5

Enhance the use of enabling technology, in particular information and communications technology, to promote the empowerment of women

Related Agenda 2063 target:

i   Mobile penetration rate.

Mobile technology is fast becoming an important tool for promoting women's empowerment, given that it expands knowledge and information available to women. Mobile phones are increasingly being used to disseminate information relating to health, education and economic empowerment. However, gender disparities exist in access to mobile technology. Ownership of a mobile account was lower among women (10.3 per cent) compared with men (12.8 per cent) in Africa (excluding North Africa) (see FIGURE 5.9).

5.5 Conclusion

The analysis of the data on the indicators for Sustainable Development Goal 5 shows that, although much progress has been made towards attaining gender equality in Africa, much more remains to be done to empower women and reduce gender disparities. As greater numbers of women are seeking education and entering the labour force, leveraging their productive contributions for economic growth and sustainable development must be prioritized. Unless gender disparities are addressed urgently, women's potential contributions to economic growth will remain untapped. Translating policy commitments into action remains a challenge. Greater efforts are needed to strengthen laws, improve public services and enhance women's representation in leadership and their access to resources. Furthermore, data limitations pose a significant constraint to monitoring progress and evaluating the impact of policy commitments on gender. Strengthening data availability will be critical to assessing the achievements under Goal 5.

Unless gender disparities are addressed urgently, women's potential contributions to economic growth will remain untapped.

CHAPTER 6

Goal 9:
Industry, innovation and infrastructure

6.1 Introduction

Sustainable Development Goal 9, to build resilient infrastructure, promote inclusive and sustainable industrialization and foster innovation, addresses three important aspects of sustainable development: infrastructure, industrialization and innovation. Infrastructure provides the basic physical facilities essential to business and societal development; industrialization drives economic growth and decent job creation, thereby reducing income poverty; and innovation expands the technological capabilities of industrial sectors and leads to the development of new skills. The Goal is aimed at consolidating national and international efforts towards promoting infrastructure development, industrialization and innovation. Achieving this requires increased domestic and international financial mobilization, technological and technical support, research and innovation, and increased access to information and communication technology. Goal 9 is one of the most critical Goals in support of Africa's aspiration for rapid development and transformation through increased productive capacities. Achieving the Goal will have positive multiplier effects for all other Goals.

Sustainable Development Goal 9, to build resilient infrastructure, promote inclusive and sustainable industrialization and foster innovation, addresses three important aspects of sustainable development: infrastructure, industrialization and innovation.

6.2 Targets and alignment with Agenda 2063

Sustainable Development Goal 9 has 8 targets and 12 indicators and is aligned with 7 goals of Agenda 2063. The areas of sustainable development underscored in this Goal are also covered in goal 1 (a high standard of living, quality of life and well-being for all); goal 4 (transformed economies and job creation); goal 5 (modern agriculture for increased productivity and production); goal 6 (blue/ocean economy for accelerated economic growth); goal 8 (united Africa (federal or confederate));

goal 10 (world-class infrastructure criss-crosses Africa); and goal 19 (Africa as a major partner in global affairs and peaceful coexistence) of Agenda 2063 (see TABLE 6.1). Priority area 2 of goal 4, namely, science, technology and innovation-driven manufacturing, industrialization and value addition, covers issues of industrialization and innovation, and priority area of goal 10 is focused exclusively on infrastructure.

SDG 9 TARGETS	AGENDA 2063 GOALS 1, 4, 5, 6, 7, 8, 10, AND 19* TARGETS
9.1 Develop quality, reliable, sustainable and resilient infrastructure, including regional and trans-border infrastructure, to support economic development and human well-being, with a focus on affordable and equitable access for all	**1.1.4.8** At least detail technical and financial feasibility report for rapid transit system for all cities above 2 million people is completed.
	1.1.4.11 All settlements in Small Island States are linked by frequent, efficient and effective, (where appropriate) land, air and sea rapid transit systems by 2020
	1.4.3.4 Level of intra-African trade in agricultural commodities is increased by at least 100% in real terms.
	1.4.3.5 Level of intra African trade in services is increased by at least 100% in real terms
	1.4.4.3 2013 Level of intra-African tourism is doubled in real terms
	1.5.1.8 Triple intra African Trade of agricultural commodities and services
	1.6.2.2 Locally, owned shipping lines carry at least 5% of annual tonnage of cargo
	2.8.1.5 Volume of intra-African trade is at least three times the 2013 level
	2.8.1.6 Volume of trade with African Island States is increased by at least 10%
	2.10.1.1 At least national readiness for implementation of the trans African Highway Missing link is achieved
	2.10.1.2 At least national readiness for in country connectivity to the African High Speed Rail Network is achieved by 2019
	2.10.1.3 Skies fully opened to African airlines
9.2 Promote inclusive and sustainable industrialization and, by 2030, significantly raise industry's share of employment and gross domestic product, in line with national circumstances, and double its share in least developed countries	**1.4.1.2** At least 30% of total non-extractive sector industrial output is from locally owned firms.
	1.4.2.1 Real value of manufacturing in GDP is 50% more than the 2013 level.
	1.4.2.2 Share of labour intensive manufacturing output is 50% more than that of 2013 level
9.3 Increase the access of small-scale industrial and other enterprises, in particular in developing countries, to financial services, including affordable credit, and their integration into value chains and markets	**1.4.1.2** At least 30% of total non-extractive sector industrial output is from locally owned firms.
	1.4.1.3 At least locally owned firms generate 20% of the extractive sector industrials output.
	1.4.2.3 At least 20% of total output of the extractive industry is through value addition by locally owned firms.
9.4 By 2030, upgrade infrastructure and retrofit industries to make them sustainable, with increased resource-use efficiency and greater adoption of clean and environmentally sound technologies and industrial processes, with all countries taking action in accordance with their respective capabilities	**1.1.4.9** At least 50% of urban waste is recycled.
	1.7.3.5 All Cities meet the WHO's Ambient Air Quality Standards (AAQS) by 2025

TABLE 6.1 (CONT)

SDG 9 TARGETS	AGENDA 2063 GOALS 1, 4, 5, 6, 7, 8, 10, AND 19* TARGETS
9.5 Enhance scientific research, upgrade the technological capabilities of industrial sectors in all countries, in particular developing countries, including, by 2030, encouraging innovation and substantially increasing the number of research and development workers per 1 million people and public and private research and development spending	**1.4.2.5** Gross Domestic Expenditures on R&D (GERD) as a percentage of GDP has reached 1% by 2023
	1.4.3.6 At least 1% of GDP is allocated to science, technology and innovation research and STI driven entrepreneurship development.
	7.19.1.2 National systems/ infrastructure for research and development is fully functional
9.a Facilitate sustainable and resilient infrastructure development in developing countries through enhanced financial, technological and technical support to African countries, least developed countries, landlocked developing countries and small island developing States	**2.10.1.1** At least national readiness for implementation of the trans African Highway Missing link is achieved
	2.10.1.2 At least national readiness for in country connectivity to the African High Speed Rail Network is achieved by 2019
	2.10.1.3 Skies fully opened to African airlines
9.b Support domestic technology development, research and innovation in developing countries, including by ensuring a conducive policy environment for, inter alia, industrial diversification and value addition to commodities	**1.4.1.2** At least 30% of total non-extractive sector industrial output is from locally owned firms.
	1.4.1.3 At least locally owned firms generate 20% of the extractive sector industrials output.
	1.4.2.1 Real value of manufacturing in GDP is 50% more than the 2013 level.
	1.4.2.2 Share of labour intensive manufacturing output is 50% more than that of 2013 level
	1.4.2.3 At least 20% of total output of the extractive industry is through value addition by locally owned firms.
	1.4.2.5 Gross Domestic Expenditures on R&D (GERD) as a percentage of GDP has reached 1% by 2023
	1.4.3.1 Improvement in diversification index of 2013 is at least 20%.
	1.4.3.6 At least 1% of GDP is allocated to science, technology and innovation research and STI driven entrepreneurship development.
	7.19.1.3 Increase 2013 level of exports by 20% in real terms
9.c. Significantly increase access to information and communications technology and strive to provide universal and affordable access to the Internet in least developed countries by 2020	**2.10.1.8** Attain 100% mobile penetration by 2020
	1.1.4.6 Access and use of electricity and internet is increased by at least 50% of 2013 levels
	2.10.1.5 Double ICT penetration and contribution to GDP
	2.10.1.6 Realize at least 70% increase in broadband accessibility by 2020
	2.10.1.7 Digital broadcasting is achieved as the norm by 2016
	7.19.1.2 National systems / infrastructure for research and development is fully functional

Source: Authors' own analysis based on Statistics Division (2017b) and African Union Commission (2015).

* Goal 1 (a high standard of living, quality of life and well-being for all); goal 4 (transformed economies and job creation); goal 5 (modern agriculture for increased productivity and production); and goal 7 (environmentally sustainable climate-resilient economies and communities) of aspiration 1; goal 8 (united Africa (federal or confederate)) and goal 10 (world-class infrastructure criss-crosses Africa) of aspiration 2; and goal 19 (Africa as a major partner in global affairs and peaceful coexistence) of aspiration 7.

6.3 Data availability, current status in Africa and the progress made

Notwithstanding the importance of Sustainable Development Goal 9, data availability is limited for some of the targets and indicators. Target 9.1, which focuses on infrastructure-related indicators, has data on air transport and railway infrastructures only. There are no organized data available, however, on road and maritime transport. Target 9.2, which focuses on industrialization, has data for the indicators covered. There are no data for the two indicators of target 9.3 (9.3.1 (proportion of small-scale industries in total industry value added) and 9.3.2 (proportion of small-scale industries with a loan or line of credit)). Target 9.4 has three indicators: 9.4.1 (emissions of carbon-dioxide); 9.4.2 (emissions of carbon dioxide per unit of GDP (purchasing power parity)); and 9.4.3 (emissions of carbon dioxide per unit of manufacturing value added). For the three indicators, data are available for 27 to 29 African countries, up to 2013. Target 9.5, which focuses on innovation research and technology, has data for the indicators covered. There are no data for the indicators of target 9.a. Indicators for targets 9.b and 9.c have data available.

Target 9.1 of Sustainable Development Goal 9
> Develop quality, reliable, sustainable and resilient infrastructure, including regional and trans-border infrastructure, to support economic development and human well-being, with a focus on affordable and equitable access for all

Related Agenda 2063 targets:

i   At least detail technical and financial feasibility report for rapid transit system for all cities of more than 2 million people is completed;

ii   All settlements in small island States are linked by frequent, efficient and effective, (where appropriate) land, air and sea rapid transit systems by 2020;

iii   Level of intra-African trade in agricultural commodities is increased by at least 100 per cent in real terms;

iv   Level of intra-African trade in services is increased by at least 100 per cent in real terms;

v   2013 level of intra-African tourism is doubled in real terms;

vi   Triple intra-African trade of agricultural commodities and services;

vii   Locally owned shipping lines carry at least 5 per cent of annual tonnage of cargo;

viii   Volume of intra-African trade is at least three times the 2013 level;

ix   Volume of trade with African island States is increased by at least 10 per cent

x   At least national readiness for implementation of the trans-African highway missing link is achieved;

BOX 6.1 KEY FACTS IN INDUSTRY, INNOVATION AND INFRASTRUCTURE GLOBALLY

In 2015, manufacturing value added per capita was almost $5,000 per capita annually in developed region, while it was less than $100 per capita annually in the least developed countries. Globally, energy efficiency and the use of cleaner fuels and technologies reduced carbon dioxide emissions per unit of value added by 13 per cent between 2000 and 2013. Although expenditure on research and development continues to grow globally, the poorest countries, especially those in Africa, spend a very small proportion of their GDP on such expenditure. In 2013, global investment in research and development stood at $1.7 trillion (purchasing power parity), up from $732 billion in 2000. Developed regions dedicated almost 2.4 per cent of their GDP to research and development in 2013, while the average for the least developed countries and landlocked developing countries was less than 0.3 per cent. Globally, third-generation mobile broadband covered 89 per cent of the urban population in 2015, but only 29 per cent of the rural population.

Source: United Nations (2016a).

xi At least national readiness for in country connectivity to the African high-speed rail network is achieved by 2019;

xii Skies fully opened to African airlines.

Indicators: 9.1.1 (proportion of the rural population who live within 2 km of an all-season road) and 9.1.2 (passenger and freight volumes, by mode of transport)

Quality infrastructure is an important prerequisite for the promotion of manufacturing and industrialization. It connects producers to markets in an efficient manner, thereby reducing production and distribution costs, increasing competitiveness, attracting new investors and fostering economic growth. Owing to data limitations, this chapter contains information mainly on progress made in air and rail transportation. No aggregated data is available on road and maritime transportation. Air transportation is a key component of physical infrastructure and crucial for international trade. The number of passengers carried by air transport and the volume of freight are interesting indicators of the dynamism and quality of air transportation.

FIGURES 6.1 AND 6.2 present the current status and evolution of these indicators for Africa, compared with other regions and economic groupings. They show that both air shipping and air travel remain extremely low in Africa (excluding North Africa). In 2015, the number of passengers carried by air was 45 million people, while the levels for Asia and the Pacific and Latin America and Caribbean were 23 times and 6 times higher, respectively.

On the other hand, the volume of air freight was 2,854 million tons, 23 times lower than the level in Asia and the Pacific and 2 times lower than the level in Latin America and the Caribbean. On the basis of these figures, in 2015, Africa (excluding North Africa) represented 1.3 per cent and 1.5 per cent, respectively, of world air travel and air shipping. It is nevertheless encouraging to see that both indicators have improved significantly, compared with their 2000 and 2010 levels. With regard to air freight, the increase was 25 per cent during the period 2000-2010 and 34 per cent during the period 2010-2015. For air travel, the progress was

FIGURE 6.I AIR TRANSPORT, PASSENGERS CARRIED

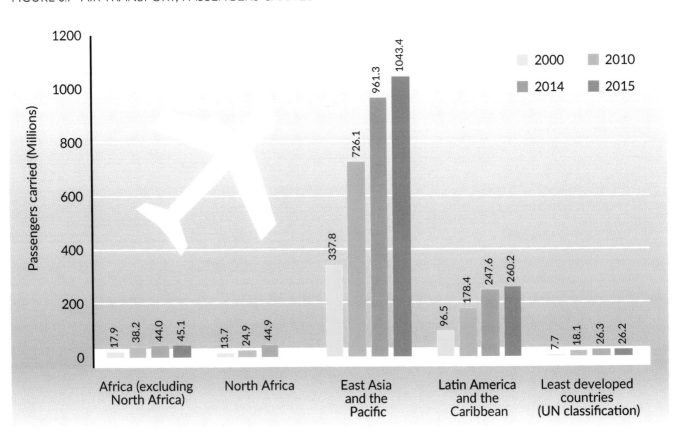

Source: Statistics Division (2017) and 2017 World Bank world development indicators.

FIGURE 6.2 AIR TRANSPORT, FREIGHT

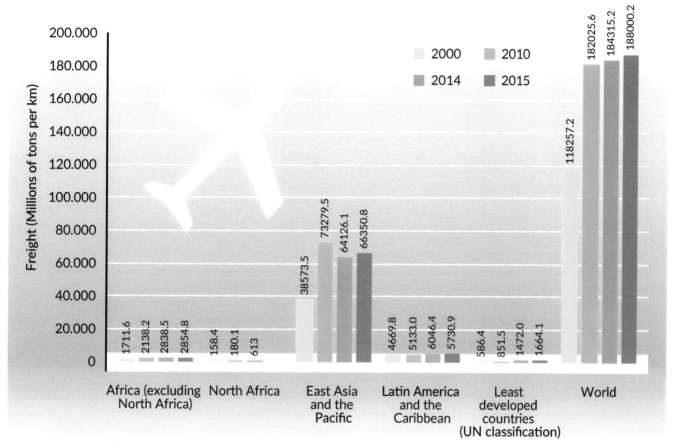

Source: Statistics Division (2017) and 2017 World Bank world development indicators.

113 per cent and 18 per cent, respectively, during the periods 2000-2010 and 2010-2015.

The overall situation masks important disparities. For example, for both indicators, the levels for the group of least developed countries (African and non-African), the 2015 levels were lower than those for Africa (excluding North Africa). This is a clear indication that African least developed countries represent an important gap in air transport infrastructure that need to be bridged if they are to become more competitive and promote industrialization faster.

With regard to North Africa, the number of passengers carried in 2014 (i.e., 44.9 million) is higher than the figure for the rest of the continent (44 million). This is likely due to the importance of tourism in the economies of North Africa. The picture is different when it comes to air shipping. Indeed, the volume of air freight in North Africa was 613 million tonnes in 2014, or six times lower than for the rest of the continent (see FIGURE 6.2). Nevertheless, North Africa has made great and steady progress in both indicators since the turn of the century. The indicator on air travel increased by

82 per cent and 80 per cent, respectively, during the periods 2000-2010 and 2010-2014. On the other hand, air freight grew by 14 per cent during the period 2000-2010 and by 240 per cent during the period 2010-2014.

Rail transportation has been a determining factor in the promotion of industrialization in advanced and emerging countries and could do the same in Africa. In the United States of America and the United Kingdom of Great Britain and Northern Ireland, for example, the advent and spread of the industrial revolution depended on the ability to transport raw materials and finished goods over long distances, to which railways contributed greatly.[1] Likewise, in India, railways are helping the economy in many ways, including by providing a fast and reliable transport medium for people and various food and non-food items (e.g., petroleum products).[2] In these countries, railroads have contributed to increasing the availability of manufactured goods and food and to a reduction in the costs

1 See http://industrialrevolutionresearch.com/ industrial_revolution_transportation.php.

2 See www.importantindia.com/10832/ importance-of-railways-in-india/.

of these products.[3] They have also contributed to the development of the rail industry through the creation of many railway-related factories, thus generating a considerable number of jobs. Railway transportation is still not very well developed in Africa. Based on 2013 data from the world development indicators database of the World Bank, in the rest of Africa, the length of rail lines amounted to 59,634 km, corresponding to 6 per cent of the total rail lines in the world. By way of comparison with other developing regions, the proportion is 12 per cent for Asia and the Pacific, 10 per cent for Latin America and the Caribbean and 3 per cent for the Middle East and North Africa.

Road transportation in Africa has the great potential to promote economic growth and lift people out of poverty. Existing information indicates, however, significant stagnation in terms of infrastructural improvement during the past decades. Average road density in Africa is only 20.4 km of road per 100 km^2 of land area, 25 per cent of which are paved. This compares poorly with the global average of 94.4 km per 100 km^2 and more than half paved. The road access rate in rural Africa is only 34 per cent (Iimi et al., 2016) compared with other developing region, 50 per cent of the population enjoy access to roads (Programme for Infrastructure Development in Africa, 2015; Gicheru and Nkem, 2017), with large variations in rural areas, for example, from 17 per cent in Zambia to 56 per cent in Kenya (Iimi et al., 2016)). Where road infrastructure exists, its quality is a big issue. According to Escribano et al. (2008), for 33 African countries, the proportion of paved roads over the total roads available was approximately 50 per cent, and for 10 African countries, this indicator was merely 10 per cent.

Target 9.2 of Sustainable Development Goal 9

Promote inclusive and sustainable industrialization and, by 2030, significantly raise industry's share of employment and gross domestic product, in line with national circumstances, and double its share in least developed countries

Related Agenda 2063 targets:

i   At least 30 per cent of total non-extractive sector industrial output is from locally owned firms;

---

3 See www2.needham.k12.ma.us/nhs/cur/Baker_00/ baker_1800_soc/baker_by_gw_p.1/railroads.htm.

ii   Real value of manufacturing in GDP is 50 per cent more than the 2013 level;

iii   Share of labour-intensive manufacturing output is 50 per cent more than that of 2013 level.

Indicator 9.2.1: manufacturing value added as a percentage of GDP

Adding value to Africa's commodities through manufacturing is essential to bring about transformation and prosperity for all, as sought in the Agenda 2063. Indeed, as experienced in other parts of the world, manufacturing is seen as having great potential for increasing productivity, creating decent jobs and thereby improving socioeconomic development prospects. Africa began the post-2015 era with a relatively low development in manufacturing, with a situation significantly better in North Africa than the rest of the continent. Manufacturing value added as a percentage of GDP stood at 10.5 per cent in Africa (excluding North Africa) and 11.3 per cent in North Africa in 2015. By comparison, the figure was 14.0 per cent in Latin America and the Caribbean and 12.6 per cent for all the least developed countries, 23 per cent for Asia and the Pacific and 16 per cent globally. Neither North Africa nor the rest of Africa made significant progress during the first half of the current decade. Manufacturing value added as a percentage of GDP increased only slightly, from 10.3 to 10.5 per cent during the period 2010-2015 for Africa (excluding North Africa) and from 11.2 to 11.5 per cent for North Africa. It is worth noting that the same indicators were 25 per cent in 2000 for Asia and the Pacific but decreased slightly since then, resulting in a total drop of 2 percentage points between 2000 and 2013.

Indicators 9.2.1 (manufacturing value added per capita) and 9.2.2 (manufacturing employment as a proportion of total employment)

Indicators 9.2.1 and 9.2.2 concern the value added per capita and employment generated by the manufacturing sector. The value added per capita in Africa illustrates the level of development of manufacturing on the continent. TABLES 6.2 and 6.3 provide information on the two indicators during the period 2005-2015. When one takes into account population size, manufacturing value addition is low but rising, especially in West, East, Central and Southern Africa as a group. In 2015, the manufacturing value added per capita was 406 in North

TABLE 6.2 MANUFACTURING VALUE ADDED PER CAPITA
(CONSTANT 2010 UNITED STATES DOLLARS)

	2005	2010	2015	VARIATION 2010-2015 (PER CENT)	VARIATION 2005-2010 (PER CENT)
North Africa	348	404	406	0.5	16.1
Africa (excluding North Africa)	139	144	165	14.6	3.6

Source: Statistics Division (2017).

TABLE 6.3 MANUFACTURING EMPLOYMENT AS A PROPORTION OF TOTAL EMPLOYMENT
(PER CENT)

	2000	2005	2010	2013	2005-2010	2000-2005
North Africa	11.9	11.2	11.9	...	6.25	-6.25
Africa (excluding North Africa)	6.1	5.6	5.4	5.4	-3.57	-8.93

Source: Statistics Division (2017).

Africa versus 165 in the rest of Africa. However, the 2015 figures reflect an improvement of 14.6 per cent for Africa (excluding North Africa) and a slight increase of 0.5 per cent for North Africa, compared with the situation in 2010.

Similarly, employment provided by the manufacturing sector is low in Africa in general, but more so in non-North African countries. Between 2010 and 2013, manufacturing employment as a proportion of total employment stagnated at 5.4 per cent in Africa (excluding North Africa). By comparison, North Africa showed a value twice as high, at 11.2 per cent in 2010 (see TABLE 6.3). It is to be noted that, unlike North Africa, manufacturing employment regressed in the rest of the continent between 2000 and 2013.

Target 9.3 of Sustainable Development Goal 9
Increase the access of small-scale industrial and other enterprises, in particular in developing countries, to financial services, including affordable credit, and their integration into value chains and markets

Related Agenda 2063 targets:

i   At least 30 per cent of total non-extractive sector industrial output is from locally owned firms;

ii At least locally owned firms generate 20 per cent of the extractive sector industrials output;

iii At least 20 per cent of total output of the extractive industry is through value addition by locally owned firms.

Indicator 9.3.1: proportion of small-scale industries in total industry value added

There are no data on this indicator.

Target 9.4 of Sustainable Development Goal 9

By 2030, upgrade infrastructure and retrofit industries to make them sustainable, with increased resource-use efficiency and greater adoption of clean and environmentally sound technologies and industrial processes, with all countries taking action in accordance with their respective capabilities

Currently, Africa as a region spends less than half of 1 per cent of its GDP on research and development, compared with more than 1 per cent in the developing region as a whole and 2 per cent in the developed regions. This has adverse implications for innovation in and the transformation of African countries.

Related Agenda 2063 targets:

i At least 50 per cent of urban waste is recycled;

ii All cities meet the World Health Organization ambient air quality standards by 2025.

The indicators for this target refer mainly to the quality of production systems, especially in the manufacturing sector, and assess the extent to which they are polluting. Given that it is at a very early stage of its industrial development process, it is timely for Africa to critically examine its capacity to promote sustainable industries and sustainable development.

Indicators 9.4.1 (emissions of carbon dioxide) and 9.4.2 (emissions of carbon dioxide per unit of GDP (purchasing power parity))

From the available evidence, Africa's contributions to carbon-dioxide emissions remains negligible. In 2013, all African countries combined produced slightly more than 1,000 metric tons of CO_2, a negligible fraction of the global emissions equivalent of more than 32,000 metric tons. With respect to emissions of carbon dioxide per unit of GDP (purchasing power parity), Africa contributes some 0.2 units, compared with the

BOX 6.2 PROMOTION OF RENEWABLE ENERGY IN MOROCCO

Morocco is making significant efforts towards the promotion of renewable energy, which will contribute to making industries more sustainable, with increased resource-use efficiency. Its national energy strategy has two important objectives:

- By 2020, ensure that 44 per cent of installed electrical power comes from renewable sources, of which 2000 MW is solar power, 2000 MW wind power and 2000 MW hydro power

- Achieve efficiency in energy by saving 12 per cent of energy in 2020 and 15 per cent in 2030, mainly in the building, industry and transportation sectors

The first solar complex, NOOR I, with a capacity of 500 MW, was established in Ouarzazate in June 2013. The first delivery of electricity from this complex was planned for the end of 2015. Subsequent phases are NOOR II and NOOR III.

In addition, Morocco plans to pursue targeted programmes for environmental upgrading and an improvement in citizens' living conditions through its national strategy for sustainable development, which will transform the country's commitments into sustainable development.

Source: Government of Morocco (2015).

global 0.3 units per unit of GDP. Although low emissions in Africa may appear to be a positive development, it obviously stems from the low level of industrial development of the continent. Nevertheless, as a late-comer to the industrialization process, there is room to find ways of decoupling high carbon emission from industrial development through the adoption of new technologies and renewable energies. Morocco offers a good example in this area (see BOX 6.2).

Target 9.5 of Sustainable Development Goal 9

> Enhance scientific research, upgrade the technological capabilities of industrial sectors in all countries, in particular developing countries, including, by 2030, encouraging innovation and substantially increasing the number of research and development workers per 1 million people and public and private research and development spending

Related Agenda 2063 targets:

i   Gross expenditure on research and development as a percentage of GDP has reached 1 per cent by 2023;

ii At least 1 per cent of GDP is allocated to science, technology and innovation research and entrepreneurship development driven by science, technology and innovation;

iii National systems/infrastructure for research and development is fully functional.

Indicators 9.5.1 (research and development expenditure as a proportion of GDP) and 9.5.2 (researchers (in full-time equivalent) per million inhabitants)

Advances in scientific and technological knowledge through research are critical to eradicating poverty and promoting home-grown economic and social development. Knowledge expansion and up-to-date data provide countries with the tools to address emerging challenges.

Currently, Africa as a region spends less than half of 1 per cent of its GDP on research and development, compared with more than 1 per cent in the developing region as a whole and 2 per cent in the developed regions. This has adverse implications for innovation in and the transformation of African countries. During the period 2000-2013, Africa's expenditure on research and development as a share of GDP marginally increased, by 0.23 per cent, in North Africa and 0.01 per cent in the rest of Africa. Regardless of the marginal increases in Africa, the figures are substantially lower than those of other groups of countries. In 2013, developed countries registered increases of 2.36 per cent, developing countries 1.16 per cent and the world as a whole 1.70 per cent. A similar trend is also observed for Africa in terms of the number of full-time researchers. In particular, Africa (excluding North Africa) had 95 full-time researchers per 1 million inhabitants in 2013, while other groups had more researchers in place. Developed countries had 3,641 researchers per 1 million inhabitants, developing countries 536 researchers and the world in general 1,083 researchers.

Undoubtedly, robust spending on research and development is required for African countries, and, given the underperformance, aligning strategically with development targets is essential in order to pursue sustainable development goals.

Target 9.a of Sustainable Development Goal 9

> Facilitate sustainable and resilient infrastructure development in developing countries through enhanced financial, technological and technical support to African countries, least developed countries, landlocked developing countries and small island developing State

Related Agenda 2063 targets:

i   At least national readiness for implementation of the trans-African highway missing link is achieved;

ii At least national readiness for in-country connectivity to the African high-speed rail network is achieved by 2019;

iii Skies fully opened to African airlines.

During the period 2001-2006, Africa financed less than half (i.e. $43 billion) of its annual infrastructure needs of $93 billion, resulting in an annual deficit of $50 billion.

FIGURE 6.3 DONORS TO AFRICA'S INFRASTRUCTURE, 2008-2010

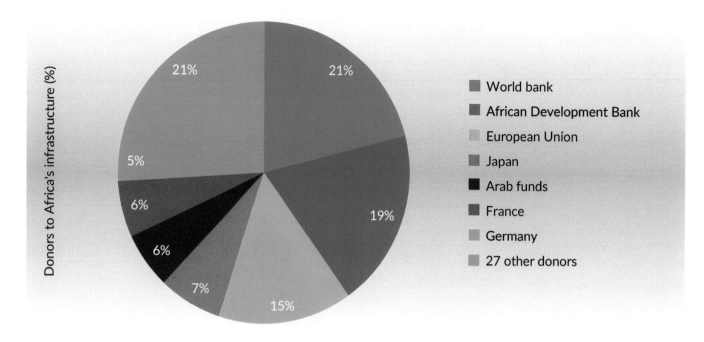

Source: Organization for Economic Cooperation and Development, 2012.

Indicator 9.a.1: total official international support (official development assistance plus other official flows) to infrastructure

During the period 2001-2006, Africa financed less than half (i.e. $43 billion) of its annual infrastructure needs of $93 billion, resulting in an annual deficit of $50 billion. Approximately two-thirds of Africa's infrastructure spending is domestically resourced, from governments and private sector; the latter contributing around 20% of that spending. FIGURE 6.3 illustrates the contribution of donors to Africa's infrastructure funding. During the period 2008-2010, multilateral organizations consisting of the World Bank, AfDB and the European Union provided more than half the official development financing (ODA plus non-concessional funds). Among the bilateral donors, the highest contributions came from Japan, France and Germany and the Arab States.

Increased mobile phone connectivity in Africa is a major source of information and social interaction; it also contributes to creating a platform for innovation in the business sector.

Target 9.b: of Sustainable Development Goal 9

Support domestic technology development, research and innovation in developing countries including by ensuring a conducive policy environment for, inter alia, industrial diversification and value addition to commodities

Related Agenda 2063 targets:

i   At least locally owned firms generate 20 per cent of the extractive sector industrials output;

ii At least 30 per cent of total non-extractive sector industrial output is from locally owned firms;

iii Real value of manufacturing in GDP is 50 per cent more than the 2013 level. Share of labour-intensive manufacturing output is 50 per cent more than that of 2013 level;

iv At least 20 per cent of total output of the extractive industry is through value addition by locally owned firms;

v   Gross expenditure on research and development as a percentage of GDP has reached 1 per cent by 2023;

vi Improvement in diversification index of 2013 is at least 20 per cent;

vii At least 1 per cent of GDP is allocated to science, technology and innovation research and entrepreneurship development driven by science, technology and innovation;

viii Increase 2013 level of exports by 20 per cent in real terms.

Indicator 9.b.1: proportion of medium-tech and high-tech industry value added in total value added

Data for this indicator are available for 29 African countries. Based on the most recent data (i.e., 2013), the proportion of medium-tech and high-tech industry value added in total value added is on average only 0.1 per cent for all African countries with data. This is extremely low, compared with approximately 0.5 per cent for developed countries such as the United Kingdom and the United States. These figures have remained the same since 2010, and for six countries the ratio is zero.

Target 9.c of Sustainable Development Goal 9

Significantly increase access to information and communications technology and strive to provide universal and affordable access to the Internet in least developed countries by 2020

Related Agenda 2063 targets:

i Attain 100 per cent mobile penetration by 2020;

ii Access and use of electricity and Internet is increased by at least 50 per cent, compared with 2013 levels;

iii National systems/ infrastructure for research and development is fully functional;

iv Double information and communications technology penetration and contribution to GDP;

v Realize at least 70 per cent increase in broadband accessibility by 2020;

vi Digital broadcasting is achieved as the norm by 2016.

Indicator: 9.c.1 proportion of population covered by a mobile network, by technology

Widespread access to broadband Internet is a key driver of economic growth, job creation and social inclusion. In addition, it serves as a transition to knowledge-intensive economies (Gelvanovska et al., 2014). Increased

mobile phone connectivity in Africa is a major source of information and social interaction; it also contributes to creating a platform for innovation in the business sector. In Kenya, for example, the mobile money platform, M-PESA, of Safaricom, is leading a business revolution, with positive implications for faster and efficient transactions and financial inclusion. In 2016, Safaricom had more than 25 million registered M-PESA subscribers (Safaricom, 2016).

In terms of the spread of mobile cellular services, Africa has made exceptional progress on higher-speed Internet access through 3G mobile broadband networks. During the past decade, the share of the population using 3G mobile networks in Africa has been converging with the rest of the world.

In 2014, 53.2 per cent of the population of Africa, excluding North Africa, had access to a 3G mobile network, comparing favourably with least developed countries (50.1 per cent), landlocked developing countries (48.7 per cent) and small island developing States (48.8 per cent), but was well below the average in developed countries (94.6 per cent) and the world (66.0 per cent). 3G broadband connectivity at affordable costs can offer a wide range of socioeconomic benefits, including access to financial services such as mobile money accounts. Consequently, policy and decision makers need to make efforts to expand the coverage to rural and remote areas in Africa where access is relatively lower.

6.4 Conclusion

The review of progress on Sustainable Development Goal 9, aligned with goals 1, 4 and 10 of Agenda 2063, highlights the relatively low levels of infrastructure, manufacture and industrial development in Africa, compared with other developing regions. Looking at historical trends, major progress was registered in infrastructure development, but manufacturing and industrial sector development stagnated in terms of contribution to both value addition and job creation.

It is indicated in the review that the continent's production systems are less polluting than the rest of the world, which can be attributed to the overall low levels of industrialization than to good performance in terms of inputs and techniques used. On a positive note, the continent's access to technology is improving significantly, with mobile network (2G and 3G) coverage growing faster and converging with the rest of the world.

For Africa, achieving Sustainable Development Goal 9 is key to improving productive capacities, reducing the continent's dependence on primary commodities and promoting job growth through value-addition. African countries and their partners therefore need to make all possible efforts for the successful achievement of Goal 9. On the basis of trends observed in the chapters and beyond, a number of recommendations can be made.

To foster industrialization, Africa needs to, among other things, develop ambitious industrial development strategies underpinned by sound policies. Depending on the country context, such strategies can be based on resources, agriculture or technology. Education systems and technical training should be geared towards the needs of the strategies adopted in order to increase manufacturing productivity, which declined from 7.3 per cent during the period 2000-2008 to 3.5 per cent during the period 2009-2014 (Economic Commission for Africa, 2017).

The continent needs to increase expenditure on research and development to levels comparable to other developing regions. In order to improve the place and role of research and development in the development process, it is important to curb brain drain and increase capacities in the areas of sciences and technology. Significantly increasing domestic resource mobilization is another urgent challenge, and improved good governance and better control over illicit financial flows could help in that area. Continuous improvements in the business environment are key to mobilizing foreign direct investment and domestic resources mobilisation for industrial development. The limited access of small and medium-sized enterprises and industries to energy and water appears to be a serious obstacle to industrial development. This situation requires special attention. Equally important is the need for countries to pay attention to international norms and standards of production and packaging. Doing so will allow African products to be more competitive and increase international demand for them. An increased focus on country comparative advantage is also important to obtain faster results in terms of industrial development

and better coordination of industrial policies within the regional economic commissions and at the continental level.

Africa also needs to be more strategic in its cooperation with the rest of the world, ensuring that it draws real benefits from every such initiative. This means ensuring effective and useful technology transfer, creating more international trade opportunities and, attracting quality foreign direct investment that are labour-intensive and create decent jobs. Following recent debates on the continued feasibility of the North Atlantic Free Trade Area led by the United States, Africa could also push for the renegotiation of its cooperation regarding the economic partnership agreements with Europe. In that respect, the coalition for South-South and triangular cooperation, which was established under decision No. 465 of the twentieth summit of the African Union, should be used to improve the outcomes of Africa's economic cooperation with its development partners.

To realize these recommendations, it is paramount that African countries strengthen the capacities of their national development planning offices. Effective planning with stronger and qualified technical teams has been an important success factor for the rapid socioeconomic development of countries such as China, Japan and Malaysia (Economic Commission for Africa, 2016).

At the continental and sub-regional levels, the many initiatives with the potential to fast-track Africa's infrastructure and industrial development should be leveraged. These include the Programme for Industrial Development in Africa under the New Partnership for Africa's Development, the Accelerated Industrial Development in Africa, the Continental Free Trade Area and the African commodity strategy led by the African Union and the tripartite free trade agreement established between the Common Market for Eastern and Southern Africa, the East African Community and the Southern African Development Community.

To foster industrialization, Africa needs to, among other things, develop ambitious industrial development strategies.

CHAPTER 7

Sustainable Development Goal 14: Life below water

7.1 Introduction

Sustainable Development Goal 14, to conserve and sustainably use the oceans, seas and marine resources for sustainable development, is aimed at promoting the conservation and sustainable use of marine and coastal ecosystems, preventing marine pollution and increasing the economic benefits to small island developing States and the least developed countries from the sustainable use of marine resources.

Coastal areas attract large populations, currently estimated at approximately 40 per cent of the global population, because of their rich resources, in particular food and other subsistence resources; access points to marine trade and transport; recreational activities; and their connection between land and sea (Neumann et al., 2015; National Oceanic and Atmospheric Administration, 2013). Around the world, population growth and rates of urbanization along the coastal

TABLE 7.1   ALIGNMENT OF SUSTAINABLE DEVELOPMENT GOAL 14 OF THE 2030 AGENDA
WITH THAT OF AGENDA 2063

TARGETS OF SUSTAINABLE DEVELOPMENT GOAL 14	TARGETS OF GOALS 4, 6 AND 7 OF AGENDA 2063*
14.1 By 2025, prevent and significantly reduce marine pollution of all kinds, in particular from land-based activities, including marine debris and nutrient pollution	**1.7.1.2** At least 17 per cent of terrestrial and inland water and 10 per cent of coastal and marine areas are preserved
14.2 By 2020, sustainably manage and protect marine and coastal ecosystems to avoid significant adverse impacts, including by strengthening their resilience, and take action for their restoration in order to achieve healthy and productive oceans	**1.7.1.2** At least 17 per cent of terrestrial and inland water and 10 per cent of coastal and marine areas are preserved
14.3 Minimize and address the impacts of ocean acidification, including through enhanced scientific cooperation at all levels	**1.7.1.2** At least 17 per cent of terrestrial and inland water and 10 per cent of coastal and marine areas are preserved
14.4 By 2020, effectively regulate harvesting, end overfishing, illegal, unreported and unregulated fishing and destructive fishing practices and implement science-based management plans in order to restore fish stocks in the shortest time feasible, at least to levels that can produce maximum sustainable yield as determined by their biological characteristics	
14.5 By 2020, conserve at least 10 per cent of coastal and marine areas, consistent with national and international law and based on the best available scientific information	**1.7.1.2** At least 17 per cent of terrestrial and inland water and 10 per cent of coastal and marine areas are preserved
14.6 By 2020, prohibit certain forms of fisheries subsidies which contribute to overcapacity and overfishing, eliminate subsidies that contribute to illegal, unreported and unregulated fishing and refrain from introducing new such subsidies, recognizing that appropriate and effective special and differential treatment for developing and least developed countries should be an integral part of the World Trade Organization fisheries subsidies negotiation	

areas are much higher compared with the hinterland owing to significant economic activity and inward migration. The global population living in low-elevation coastal zones is projected to increase from some 625 million people in 2000 to approximately 900 million by 2030 (Neumann et al., 2015). More than 3 billion people depend on fish for animal protein and some 300 million people make their livelihoods in marine fisheries (Economist, 2017; Neumann et al., 2015). The oceans play a key role in regulating the global climate and temperatures, as well as providing water and oxygen and serving as a repository for greenhouse gases.

The biggest security challenge along Africa's coastlines, especially around East Africa, is piracy.

TABLE 7.1   (CONT)

TARGETS OF SUSTAINABLE DEVELOPMENT GOAL 14	TARGETS OF GOALS 4, 6 AND 7 OF AGENDA 2063*
	1.4.4.2 Eco-friendly coastal tourism increased by 20 per cent by 2020, with at least 10 per cent of the public revenue from it going to finance development programmes of the communities
14.7 By 2030, increase the economic benefits to small island developing States and least developed countries from the sustainable use of marine resources, including through sustainable management of fisheries, aquaculture and tourism	**1.6.1.1** At least 50 per cent increase in value addition in the fishery sector in real term is attained by 2023
	1.6.1.3 Marine biotechnology contribution to GDP is increased in real terms by at least 50 per cent from the 2013 level
14.a Increase scientific knowledge, develop research capacity and transfer marine technology, taking into account the Intergovernmental Oceanographic Commission Criteria and Guidelines on the Transfer of Marine Technology, in order to improve ocean health and to enhance the contribution of marine biodiversity to the development of developing countries, in particular small island developing States and least developed countries	**1.6.1.1** At least 50 per cent increase in value addition in the fishery sector in real term is attained by 2023
14.b Provide access for small-scale artisanal fishers to marine resources and markets	
14.c Enhance the conservation and sustainable use of oceans and their resources by implementing international law as reflected in the United Nations Convention on the Law of the Sea, which provides the legal framework for the conservation and sustainable use of oceans and their resources, as recalled in paragraph 158 of "The future we want"	

Source: Authors' own analysis based on Statistics Division (2017b) and African Union Commission (2015).
* Goal 4 (transformed economies and job creation); goal 6 (blue/ocean economy for accelerated economic growth); and goal 7 (environmentally sustainable climate-resilient economies and communities) of aspiration 1.

Given the high population growth and increasing economic activity and that water is a global common resource, however, the management and optimal harvesting of underwater resources and the coastal areas in general is a challenge. For example, more than 80 per cent of marine pollution comes from the land-based surroundings. The introduction of invasive species, including through the exchange of ship ballast water, is a major concern (United Nations, 2017). Managing coastal ecosystems sustainably requires maintaining a good balance between economic use and biodiversity and habitat conservation, informed by expert scientific information and best practices. Small island developing States, in particular, suffer acutely from the degradation of marine ecosystems.

Maritime security is critical in most coastal areas. Most of the problems at sea originate on land (Smed, 2015), given that they are spearheaded by human activity. Crime, smuggling and armed attacks at sea stem from many of the same challenges as on land. Maritime security includes the protection of maritime trade, resource utilization, environmental protection and the jurisdiction of accountable authorities.

The biggest security challenge along Africa's coastlines, especially around East Africa, is piracy (African Development Bank, 2010). Piracy along the East African coast escalated during the period 2006-2008: the number of attacks off the Horn of Africa almost doubled, from 84 to 160, and hijackings increased from 5 to 44 (Smed, 2015). The good news is that recent data show a substantial decline in piracy, both in numbers and the severity of attacks: 55 piracy attacks were recorded in 2014, down from 79 in 2013. Of these, 41 occurred in the west, in the Gulf of Guinea and Atlantic Ocean seaboard, and 12 along the East African coastline (Walker, 2015).

According to Walker (2015), approximately half of the piracy incidents off the coast of Guinea are not reported. It is therefore important for coastal countries to strengthen efforts to improve data-gathering and information- sharing for accurate reporting in order to best understand the magnitude of the problem coordination efforts are needed. Other key dimensions of maritime security include terrorism and rebel activities, local crime syndicates, unresolved maritime boundary disputes and disagreements over the location and extraction of resources (Smed, 2015; Walker, 2015).

The Agenda 2063 targets are expected to be achieved through expanding knowledge of marine and aquatic biotechnology, investing more resources in developing shipping, sea, river and lake transport and developing capacity for fishing and mineral exploitation

7.2 Targets and alignment with Agenda 2063

Sustainable Development Goal 14 has 10 targets and is fully aligned with goal 6 (the blue economy for accelerated growth) of Agenda 2063 and aligned in part with goal 4 (transformed economies and job creation) and goal 7 (environmentally sustainable climate-resilient economies and communities). The preamble to goal 6 of Agenda 2063 underscores the critical importance of Africa's marine area, which is three times larger than the continental land mass, as a potential driver of economic growth and transformation. The Agenda 2063 targets are expected to be achieved through expanding knowledge of marine and aquatic biotechnology, investing more resources in developing shipping, sea, river and lake transport and developing capacity for fishing and mineral exploitation. BOX 7.1 highlights some of the key facts of life below water in the context of Africa.

BOX 7.1 KEY FACTS ABOUT LIFE BELOW WATER FOR AFRICA

At least 38 African countries are coastal States, 6 of which are island States and thus have a keen interest in the improved management of life below water. Overall, Africa has a coastline stretching approximately 40,000 km. The island of Madagascar has the longest coastline (some 4,800 km long), with Somalia (3,000 km), South Africa (2,800 km), Mozambique (2,500 km) and Egypt (2,500) having the longest beaches on the mainland

Because of the attractiveness of the coastal areas, they tend to be densely populated, with high population growth, increasing approximately 3.3 per cent annually. Africa's coastal areas have the highest population growth and urbanization rates globally. The population of Africa living in low-elevation coastal zones is projected to increase from 54 million in 2000 to approximately 100 million by 2030.

Coastal areas are therefore critical to Africa's and the world's economic growth and transformation through supporting large volumes of international trade at a low cost and improving poverty eradication, employment and tourism. Recent estimates show that more than 90 per cent of Africa's exports and imports are transported on the sea (BusinessTech, 2015), higher than the global average of approximately 80 per cent. Africa's sea ports, however, are often overcrowded owing to increasing trade that outstrips the capacity of existing facilities and managerial inefficiencies (African Development Bank, 2010). Sustained investment to expand maritime facilities and innovations that take into account the environmental implications of further development are therefore required.

The biggest risk to coastal areas is environmental degradation, which is intensified by overfishing, the destruction of coral reefs and mangroves, pollution (from plastics, oil spills, etc.) and sedimentation. Since the nineteenth century, the temperature of ocean waters has increased by 0.7 degrees Celsius, and the trend continues. Current estimates show that the sustainability of fish stocks is declining, from 70.1 per cent in 2009 to 68.6 per cent in 2013. Approximately 90 per cent of global fish stocks are fished to unsustainable levels. The impact of environmental degradation of coastal areas is worse in developing countries. Coastal populations face the risk of rising sea levels, in particular for those living in low elevation zones (at altitudes of 10 metres or less above sea level), which are likely to hit African coastal countries hard. The most recent estimates show that the total number of people at risk of coastal flooding will reach between 268 and 286 million in 2030. Africa's at-risk population is expected to double from 13 million in 2000 to 26 million by 2030.

Source: African Development Bank, (2010); Neumann et al., (2015); Economist (2017).

7.3 Data availability, current status in Africa and the progress made

While the importance of Sustainable Development Goal 14 cannot be overstated, data gaps and the lack of methodological definitions for the majority of the indicators for this Goal are significant. Only two targets, namely, 14.4.4 and 14.4.5, have indicators for which data are available with agreed methodology. Specifically, of the 10 indicators, only 2, 14.4.1 and 14.5.1, are in tier I (with data), while the rest are in tier III (see TABLE 7.2).[1]

_____

1   Tier I indicators are conceptually clear, established methodology and standards available; data are regularly produced by countries. Tier II indicators are conceptually clear, established methodology and standards available. Data are not regularly produced by countries. Tier III indicators are a work in progress. There are no established methodology and standards or methodology/ standards are being developed/ tested.

TABLE 7.2   INDICATORS OF SUSTAINABLE DEVELOPMENT GOAL 14 BY TIER OF DATA AVAILABILITY
AND METHODOLOGY DEFINITION

TARGET	INDICATOR	TIER
14.1	**14.1.1:** index of coastal eutrophication and floating plastic debris density	III
14.2	**14.2.1:** proportion of national exclusive economic zones managed using ecosystem-based approaches	III
14.3	**14.3.1:** average marine acidity (pH) measured at agreed suite of representative sampling stations	III
14.4	**14.4.1:** proportion of fish stocks within biologically sustainable levels	I
14.5	**14.5.1:** coverage of protected areas in relation to marine areas	I
14.6	**14.6.1:** progress by countries in the degree of implementation of international instruments aiming to combat illegal, unreported and unregulated fishing	III
14.7	**14.7.1:** sustainable fisheries as a percentage of GDP in small island developing States, least developed countries and all countries	III
14.a	**14.a.1:** proportion of total research budget allocated to research in the field of marine technology	III
14.b	**14.b.1:** progress by countries in the degree of application of a legal regulatory/policy/institutional framework which recognizes and protects access rights for small-scale fisheries	III
14.c	**14.c.1:** number of countries making progress in ratifying, accepting and implementing through legal, policy and institutional frameworks, ocean-related instruments that implement international law, as reflected in the United Nation Convention on the Law of the Sea, for the conservation and sustainable use of the oceans and their resources	III

Source: Statistics Division (2016).

Target 4.4 of Sustainable Development Goal 14

By 2020, effectively regulate harvesting and end overfishing, illegal, unreported and unregulated fishing and destructive fishing practices and implement science-based management plans, in order to restore fish stocks in the shortest time feasible, at least to levels that can produce maximum sustainable yield as determined by their biological characteristics

This target has no related Agenda 2063 target.

Indicator 14.4.1: proportion of fish stocks within biologically sustainable levels

Data on this indicator are available only at the global level up to 2013. According to the latest data, the sustainability of fish stocks is progressively declining, from 72.6 per cent in 2000 to 70.1 per cent in 2009

and to 68.6 per cent in 2013 (Statistics Division, 2017). The key threats to the sustainability of global fisheries include overfishing, illegal and unregulated fishing and destructive fishing practices. Subsidies to the fishing industry are receiving increased attention because of their complex relation to trade, ecological sustainability and socioeconomic development. Such practices adversely affect the ocean food chain and can lead to food insecurity and poor livelihoods (United Nations, 2017).

Target 4.5 of Sustainable Development Goal 14

By 2020, conserve at least 10 per cent of coastal and marine areas, consistent with national and international law and based on the best available scientific information

elated Agenda 2063 target:

At least 17 per cent of terrestrial and inland water and 10 per cent of coastal and marine areas are preserved.

ndicator 14.5.1: coverage of protected areas in relation to marine areas

he rest of Africa performs well in terms of marine rotected areas, compared with North Africa and much f Asia. In 2014, Africa (excluding North Africa) had 2.6 er cent coverage, compared with 0.9 per cent in North frica. For most of Asia, coverage rates range from 0.2 per ent for South Asia to 2.3 per cent for South East Asia. The igures for Africa, however, compare poorly with those of

Latin America and the Caribbean (3.1 per cent), the developing regions (4.2 per cent), Oceania (7.4 per cent) and the developed regions (12.4 per cent) (FIGURE 7.1).

For Africa, data are available for 30 of the 38 coastal countries for the years 2000, 2010 and 2016. However, the data points are the same for the three years. Of the 30 countries, 7 had a protected area coverage of more than 20 per cent in 2016, with 4, namely, Equatorial Guinea, Gabon, Mozambique and Namibia, exceeding 80 per cent (see FIGURE 7.2). Fourteen of the countries with coastal areas show zero protection coverage relative to their marine areas. This is an issue of concern, given the likely catastrophic consequences of environmental degradation of the coastal areas.

FIGURE 7.1   COVERAGE OF PROTECTED AREAS IN RELATION TO MARINE AREAS, BY REGION (2014)

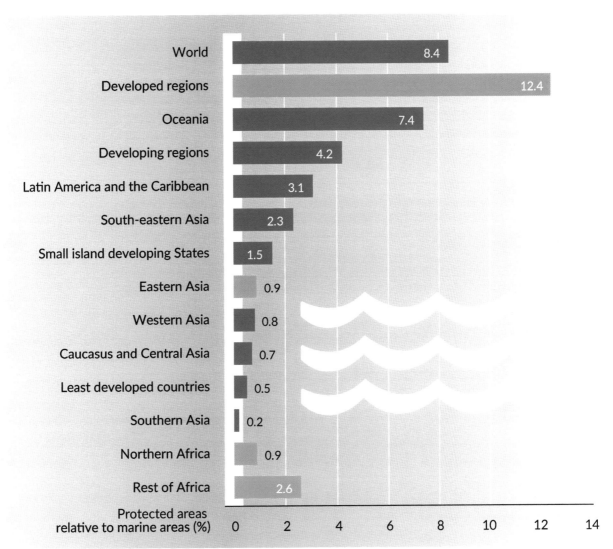

Data source: Statistics Division (2017).

FIGURE 7.2 COVERAGE OF PROTECTED AREAS, 2016

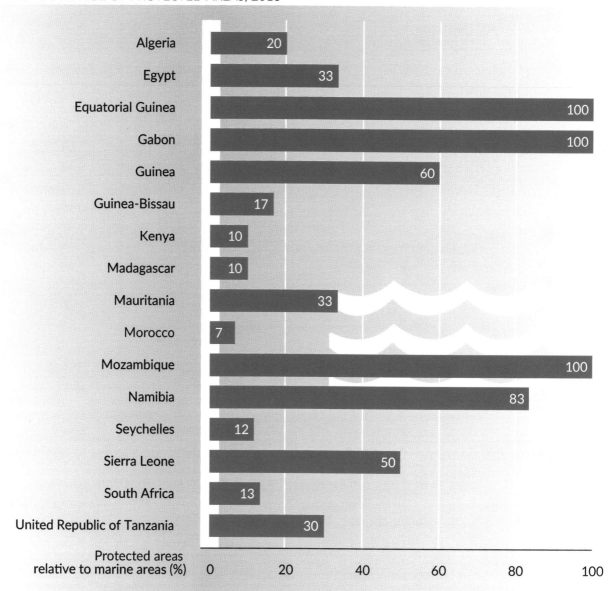

Data source: Statistics Division (2017).

7.4 Implications for small island developing States

Africa has six island States: Comoros, Madagascar, Mauritius and Seychelles in the Indian Ocean and Cabo Verde and Sao Tome and Principe in the Atlantic Ocean. Apart from Madagascar (587,000 sq. km), the rest of them are categorized as small island developing States, with a land area of less than 2,000 sq. km and of volcanic origin with low coral elevation (Shahin, 2002). The small island developing States face specific sustainable development challenges, including small populations, limited resources, vulnerability to natural disasters and external shocks, a high dependence on foreign imports and limited economies of scale. Least developed countries often share many of the same challenges. BOX 7.2 (see next page) presents some of the environmental issues in Seychelles and the Government's leadership in addressing them.

BOX 7.2 SMALL ISLAND DEVELOPING STATES ENVIRONMENTAL ISSUES: LESSONS FROM SEYCHELLES

With a population of 93,419 people in 2015 (some 200 people per sq. km) and an income per capita of $14,760 in 2015 (World Bank, 2017), Seychelles is an upper-middle-income country and one of Africa's six small island developing States. Given its unique bird species and forests, Seychelles is one of the major biodiversity areas in the world. Sustainable Development Goal 14 and goals 4, 6 and 7 of Agenda 2063 are therefore of critical importance to the island. The country is committed to combating climate change to promote sustainable development. With a birth rate of 18.1 per 1,000 people annually, an economic growth rate of about 3.5 per cent annually in 2015 and tourism arrivals growing at approximately 9.4 per cent during the period 2011-2016 (303,177 visitors in 2016, compared with 194,476 in 2011), the pressure of human activity on land, beachfront property, water, food and energy in the fragile and resource-scare country is expected to increase significantly by 2020.

Sustainable development is enshrined in the constitution, and the country aims to be a global leader in sustainable development. The sustainable development strategy for the period 2012-2020 presents a vision of realizing national economic, social and cultural potential through innovative, knowledge-led approaches, while conserving the integrity of the natural environment and heritage for present and future generations. The strategy includes 13 priorities, among them, sustainable social and human development, water sanitation and waste management, land use, coastal zones and urbanization, a green economy and climate change. The Ministry of Environment and Energy and all other ministries with a relevant portfolio take coordinated responsibility for the implementation of the strategy.

Seychelles was one of the first countries in the western Indian Ocean region to designate marine protected areas. Thanks to sustained efforts, the country has 47 per cent of its territory under legal protection. Between 1995 and 2000, Seychelles sequestered more than 800 gigagrams of greenhouse gas emissions, making the country a net repository, notwithstanding the 34 per cent increase in carbon dioxide gas emissions, in particular due to the increased use of oil for electricity generation. Among the mitigation measures employed is the 18 MW wind energy farm completed in 2012.

Given the scale of the challenges, however, the resources required to maintain a comprehensive programme of environmental regulation are limited. The threats to a loss of biodiversity and the natural environment due to human activities and the consequences of climate change and biological invasions require close monitoring. The majority of the country's coral reefs were infected by the mass coral bleaching of 1998 due to the unexpected warming of the waters following El Niño. Seychelles has no natural fresh water resources. Fish migration due to sea temperature changes is expected to adversely affect the tuna fish industry. Extended droughts are affecting the bird and tortoise populations. Coastal erosion due to rising sea levels and extreme weather partners affect nesting grounds for turtles and coastal infrastructure. In addition, the nation faces large water pollution challenges from industrial by-products and sewage. The Government is considering a policy to burn the use of plastics in the country.

Monitoring the environment is complicated by the large number of islands (115 altogether) distributed over a surface area of 1.3 million sq. km. All the islands put together result in a total coastline of close to 500 sq. km, with surrounding coral reefs reaching close to 1,700 sq. km.

Source: Government of Seychelles, (2012); (2013); National Bureau of Statistics (2017).

Efforts at every level, namely, the community, national, regional and international levels, are required to ensure their sustainability. Unfortunately, this is one of the Sustainable Development Goals for which data gaps to measure progress are large.

7.5 Conclusion

The world's oceans and the seas play a critical role in supporting populations, economic activity and regulating the global climate. Environmental degradation and the risk of flooding are the main challenges to the oceans and coastal areas. Efforts at every level, namely, the community, national, regional and international levels, are required to ensure their sustainability. Unfortunately, this is one of the Sustainable Development Goals for which data gaps to measure progress are large. Life below water and climate change are areas requiring concerted international effort to generate baselines for effective reporting.

Coastal national Governments, with the support the international community, need to do more to mitigate the impact of population pressure and economic activities on the coastal habitats through better coordinated planning and research. Such measures could include the following:

A Stronger coordination among the coastal countries, which will help to develop and implement integrated coastal zones and ocean management programmes;

B Good planning for population growth, economic activities and residential establishment consistent with the vulnerabilities of the coastal areas and contingency preparations to deal with the rising temperatures and sea levels;

C Further research to understand and develop resilience, as well as coping mechanisms to population living in low-lying zones;

D Strengthened technical capacity of coastal countries to deal with the environmental degradation.

Action by the international community is required to define property rights and responsibilities for additional investment and protection of the global commons problem. Most waters are outside national jurisdictions and therefore require international coordination and action to ensure their protection. The United Nations Ocean Conference, held from 5 to 9 June 2017, which focused on Sustainable Development Goal 14, was aimed at discussing measures to address marine population, conserving and restoring marine and coastal ecosystems, addressing ocean acidification, making fisheries sustainable and expanding scientific knowledge and marine technology. Such efforts need to be strengthened and resources mobilized to implement the recommendations.

The African Climate Policy Centre of ECA is spearheading support for the African small island developing States to review their vulnerabilities to the adverse effects of climate change and develop response strategies to reduce population exposure. These efforts need to be supported by member countries and other development partners.

CHAPTER 8

Conclusion and recommendations

8.1 Conclusion

In line with the theme of the 2017 high-level political forum on sustainable development, the 2017 regional report on Agenda 2063 and the 2030 Agenda focused on the following six Sustainable Development Goals: Goal 1 (No poverty), Goal 2 (Zero hunger), Goal 3 (Good health and well-being), Goal 5 (Gender equality), Goal 9 (Industry, innovation and infrastructure) and Goal 14 (Life below water). Both Agendas provide a framework to galvanize global and regional support for the realization of national priorities, drawing on the collective action of all stakeholders. Incorporating both Agendas into national development frameworks and plans, as well as designing mechanisms for monitoring and reporting progress, should therefore be the first business of all African Governments.

The report began with an analysis of the daunting data deficits that haunt the effective implementation and monitoring of country-level performance on the two Agendas. Data deficits stem largely from weak national statistical systems, limited prioritization of and funding for statistics and a lack of political will. The report's authors find that growth in Africa has not been inclusive, thereby resulting in a slow decline in poverty. Poverty, especially in West, East, Southern and Central Africa as a group, remains widespread, with large inter-country and intra-country inequalities. Similarly, food insecurity remains a major challenge in many African countries, fuelled in part by limited investment in agriculture and low agricultural productivity. Nevertheless,

> The effective implementation of both Agendas will require strengthening capacities for data-gathering, analysis and reporting. A robust data base is also vital for evidence-based policymaking.

substantial progress has been made in reducing child and maternal deaths, in part as a result of increased access to skilled birth attendants and a decline in adolescent child births. There is also evidence of improvements in the empowerment of women gauged in terms of parity in primary and secondary school enrolment and increased representation in national parliaments. However, progress has been slowed by the persistence of discriminatory cultural norms that reinforce practices such as female genital mutilation. Manufacturing and value addition in most African economies remains weak owing in part to limited infrastructure. This has contributed to limited job growth and a high prevalence of vulnerable jobs and working poor, in particular among women and young people.

The effective implementation of both Agendas will require strengthening capacities for data-gathering, analysis and reporting. A robust data base is also vital for evidence-based policymaking. Some of the data, including on poverty and inequality, that are generated through national surveys take too long to update, limiting timely and informed policy decisions.

> Both Agendas provide a framework to galvanize global and regional support for the realization of national priorities, drawing on the collective action of all stakeholders.

8.2 Recommendations

A harmonized and integrated approach to Agenda 2063 and the 2030 Agenda is required

The integrated nature of Agenda 2063 and the 2030 Agenda calls for an integrated approach to their implementation and reporting. This will avoid duplication of effort and promote coherence in policy design and implementation.

Address poverty and inequality in tandem

Efforts to reduce poverty are linked with and should be aligned with goal 10 of Agenda 2063. Studies have shown that reducing inequality by improving the livelihoods of the poorest and most vulnerable helps to reduce poverty faster. Policies on job creation, increasing household income, securing property rights, advancing infrastructure development and enhancing human capital and labour productivity are important for promoting inclusiveness, reducing poverty and ensuring inclusive growth.

Address remaining gender gaps

It is essential to address gaps in school enrolment and completion, especially at the secondary and tertiary levels, and eliminate child marriages and female genital mutilation. Strengthening law enforcement, quality of public services and increasing awareness of the advantages of equal engagement will help to further progress on gender equality. The social mores and traditions and structural constraints that impose obstacles to women's empowerment need to be addressed in order to improve women's quality of life and social development.

Increase investments in agriculture

This is urgently needed to contain extreme hunger, promote food security and support agro-processing industries and export trade. Notwithstanding the commitments for targeted investment in agriculture under the Maputo Protocol, the sector remains highly underinvested. No African sub-region met the target of allocating 10 per cent of the national budget to agriculture. Increased investment in research and development for climate-resistant breeds and appropriate technology, irrigation and developing value chains, as well as other proactive measures, such as investor-friendly policies and regulations, are required to expand both agricultural output and productivity.

Expand employment opportunities

With the rapid population growth and a rising population of young people in most Africa countries, capacity development and skills training to enhance employment opportunities are needed more than ever. More attention to labour-intensive sectors, such as agriculture and processing, is needed to promote employment and to reduce poverty and inequality faster, compared with growth in capital-intensive and skilled-labour-intensive sectors such as mining, finance and real estate.

Promote trade

Africa's share of global merchandise exports remains low, at approximately 2.4 per cent in 2015. While the unfavourable commodity prices, which dominate the bulk of Africa's exports, are in part responsible for this, Africa can do more to benefit from the ever-growing international value chain. Eliminating internal and external barriers to trade, including infrastructure bottlenecks and tariffs and promoting technology transfer and skills acquisition are vital enablers of trade competitiveness. In this regard, strengthening intra-regional trade and South-South cooperation can be useful for sharing experiences and introducing new products to less competitive markets. Stronger regional integration and regional development forums are key to supporting trade among countries of the South.

Expand fiscal space for equitable spending

To realize the breadth and depth of both Agendas, it is important for African Governments to design measures to expand fiscal space. Some of the areas to consider include improving tax administration; broadening the tax base; eliminating loopholes for tax avoidance, especially among the rich; prioritizing expenditure with the biggest impact on the less privileged (especially education, health, water and sanitation and social protection); monitoring the reach of public spending to its intended beneficiaries; and fighting illicit financial flows. Domestic borrowing for critical priority spending, such as education, health and infrastructure development, should be considered as a first option. Concessional external financing and debt issuance should also be sought for large investment.

Strengthen capacity and systems for data-gathering and management

For timely policy decisions and adequate comparison within and between countries, the national statistics offices throughout the continent require a stronger capacity for gathering and analysing data on a broad range of issues. It is important to generate data for baselines and to continuously analyse the impact of different macroeconomic and microeconomic policies on, among others, trends in poverty and inequality, education, health, labour and social protection. In addition, it is also important to analyse expenditure on various sectors of the economies and their impact on overall economic growth and progress in reducing poverty and inequality. Disaggregated data by age, gender, income and geographical location are needed to ensure an accurate assessment of the progress made in various areas and the identification and categorization of gaps and issues so that they can be addressed by the relevant authorities. The national statistical offices, supported by development partners, need to strengthen their statistics development systems and data-gathering plans in support of the reporting requirements of both Agendas.

Apply a harmonized framework for monitoring progress

To be able to measure the impact efficiently and effectively, Governments require a harmonized framework for monitoring and reporting progress on both Agendas. At present, several tools attempting to provide such measures including the mainstreaming, acceleration and policy support strategy, which is aimed at localizing the Sustainable Development Goals into national development plans, but it does not include Agenda 2063; the policy coherence for sustainable development toolkit, which is aimed at identifying clear targets and international community accountability for the Goals; and the integrated green economy implementation programme, which supports planning for green economies at national and sub-national levels. A dynamic platform or toolkit that helps to first assess the degree of integration between both Agendas, on the one hand, and the national development plans, on the other, and at the same time lends itself to measuring progress on the two frameworks, is needed.

Strengthen institutions

Successful implementation of both Agendas requires an effective institutional architecture for an integrated and coordinated approach to problem-solving and policymaking. The role of stronger and capable national and subnational planning agencies and personnel is paramount in ensuring that the various sectors work together to ensure that the three dimensions of sustainable development are reflected in all aspects of development programming. Long-term planning and policy coordination and ongoing advancements in monitoring progress, as well as impact evaluations, are needed to identify what works and to address policy failures and gaps.

Prioritize quality infrastructure development

Quality infrastructure is an important prerequisite for trade, manufacturing and industrialization. Improvements in air, marine, rail and road transportation systems and interconnections throughout the continent will help to spur economic growth through increased trade. Given the high cost of such investments, a regional approach to infrastructure design and funding is needed. Such an approach should pool funding among beneficiary countries to invest in regional public goods such as road and energy infrastructure.

References

African Development Bank (2010). *African Development Report 2010*. Tunis.

African Union (2003). Protocol to the African Charter on Human and People's Rights on the Rights of Women in Africa. Available from www.un.org/en/africa/osaa/pdf/au/protocole_rights_women_africa_2003.pdf.

_____ (2004). Solemn Declaration on Gender Equality in Africa. Available from www.un.org/en/africa/osaa/pdf/au/declaration_gender_equality_2004.pdf

African Union, Economic Commission for Africa, African Development Bank and United Nations Development Programme (2016). *MDGs to Agenda 2063/SDGs Transition Report 2016: Towards an Integrated and Coherent Approach to Sustainable Development in Africa*. Addis Ababa: Economic Commission for Africa.

African Union Commission (2015). African gender scorecard. Available from https://www.au.int/web/sites/default/files/documents/31260-doc-2015_auc_african_gender_scorecard_en.pdf.

_____ (2015). Agenda 2063: the Africa we want. A shared strategic framework for inclusive growth and sustainable development. First ten-year implementation plan 2014–2023. Available from www.un.org/en/africra/osaa/pdf/au/agenda2063-first10yearimplementation.pdf.

_____ (2016). African gender scorecard.

Basinga, P., Gertler P.J., Binagwaho, A., Soucat, A.L.B., Sturdy, J., Vermeersch, C.M.J. (2011). Effect on maternal and child health services in Rwanda of payment to primary health-care providers for performance: an impact evaluation. *The Lancet*, vol. 377, No. 9775, pp. 1421-1428.

BusinessTech (2015). Africa's biggest shipping ports, 8 March. Available from https://businesstech.co.za/news/general/81995/africas-biggest-shipping-ports/.

Cassidy, Megan. (2014). Assessing gaps in indicator availability and coverage. Sustainable Development Solutions Network

Center for Global Development (2014). Delivering on the data revolution in Sub-Saharan Africa.

Digital Globe, (2015). Transforming our world: geospatial information key to achieving the 2030 Agenda for Sustainable Development.

Economic Commission for Africa (2008). Report of the Economic Commission for Africa to the Statistical Commission, thirty-ninth session, 26-29 February 2008. Available from https://unstats.un.org/unsd/statcom/doc08/2008-14-ECA-E.pdf.

_____ (2010). Reference regional strategic framework for statistical capacity building in Africa. Addis Ababa.

_____ (2013). Report of the Economic Commission for Africa to the Statistical Commission, forty-fourth session, 26 February-1 March 2013. Available from https://unstats.un.org/unsd/statcom/doc13/2013-14-ECA-E.pdf.

_____ (2016). Planning for Africa's development: lessons, insights and messages from past and present experiences. Addis Ababa.

_____ (2017). *Economic Report on Africa 2017: Urbanisation and Industrialization for Africa's Transformation*. Addis Ababa.

Economic Commission for Africa and African Union Commission (2014). Assessment report on the 2010 round of population and housing census in Africa. Available from www.uneca.org/sites/default/files/uploaded-documents/Statistics/statcom2014/assessment_report_on_2010_round_of_census_edited_en.pdf.

Economic Commission for Africa, African Union Commission, African Development Bank and United Nations Development Programme (2015). Africa data consensus. Addis Ababa: Economic Commission for Africa. Available from www.uneca.org/sites/default/files/PageAttachments/final_adc_-_english.pdf.

_____ (2016) *MDGs to Agenda 2063/SDGs Transition Report 2016: Towards an Integrated and Coherent Approach to Sustainable Development in Africa*. Joint annual publication of the Economic Commission for Africa, African Development Bank, African Union Commission and United Nations Development Programme.

Economic Commission for Africa and Organization for Economic Cooperation and Development, (2014). The mutual review of development effectiveness in Africa: promise and performance. Economic Commission for Africa and Organization for Economic Co-operation and Development.

Economic Commission for Africa, United Nations Development Programme, OpenData and World Wide Web Foundation (2016). The Africa data revolution report 2016: highlighting developments in African data ecosystems. Addis Ababa: Economic Commission for Africa. Available from www.uneca.org/sites/default/files/uploaded-documents/ACS/africa-data-revolution-report-2016.pdf.

Economist (2017). How to improve the health of the ocean, 27 May. Available from www.economist.com/news/leaders/21722647-ocean-sustains-humanity-humanity-treats-it-contempt-how-improve-health.

Food and Agriculture Organization of the United Nations (2009). Rapid assessment of aid flows for agricultural development in sub-Saharan Africa. Investment Centre Division Discussion Paper. Available from www.fao.org/3/a-bq476e.pdf.

_____ (2014). Area equipped for irrigation. Available from www.fao.org/nr/water/aquastat/infographics/Irrigation_eng.pdf.

_____ (2016). Ethiopia situation report - April 2016. Available from http://www.fao.org/emergencies/resources/documents/resources-detail/en/c/410229/.

Gelvanovska, N., Rogy, M. and Rossotto, C.M. (2014). Broadband Networks in the Middle East and North Africa: Accelerating High-Speed Internet Access. Washington, D.C.: World Bank.

Girls Not Brides (2015). Ending child marriage in Africa. Policy Brief. Available from http://www.girlsnotbrides.org/wp-content/uploads/2015/02/Child-marriage-in-Africa-A-brief-by-Girls-Not-Brides.pdf.

Government of Morocco (2015). Morocco between the Millennium Development Goals and Sustainable Development Goals: achievements and challenges. National report 2015.

Government of Seychelles, (2012). National preparations for the United Nations Conference for Sustainable Development, Rio 2012. Available from https://sustainabledevelopment.un.org/content/documents/1019Seychelles%20National%20Report.pdf.

_____ (2013). Seychelles sustainable development strategy 2012-2020 (Vol. 1). Available from www.egov.sc/edoc/pubs/frmpubdetail.aspx?pubId=26.

IAEG, (2016) Report of the Inter-Agency and Expert Group on Sustainable Development. Goal Indicators to Statistical Commission, Forty-seventh session, 8 - 11 March 2016. Available at: https://unstats.un.org/sdgs/files/meetings/iaeg-sdgs-meeting-05/2017-2-IAEG-SDGs-E.pdf

Independent Expert Advisory Group on the Data Revolution for Sustainable Development (2014). A world that counts: mobilising the fata revolution for sustainable development. Available from www.undatarevolution.org/wp-content/uploads/2014/11/A-World-That-Counts.pdf.

International Labour Organization (2015). *World Employment Social Outlook: The Changing Nature of Jobs*. Geneva. Available from www.ilo.org/wcmsp5/groups/public/---dgreports/---dcomm/---publ/documents/publication/wcms_368626.pdf.

_____ (2016). *World Employment Social Outlook: Trends 2016*. Geneva.

International Monetary Fund (2015). *World Economic Outlook: Adjusting to World Commodity Prices*. Washington, D.C.

_____ (2016). Inequality, gender gaps and economic growth: comparative evidence for sub-Saharan Africa. Working Paper, WP/16/111. Washington, D. C.

_____ (2016). World economic outlook: a shifting global economic landscape. January 2017 update. Washington, D.C.

Kiregyera, Ben (2015). *The Emerging Data Revolution in Africa: Strengthening the Statistics, Policy and Decision-making Chain*. SUN MeDIA Stellenbosch.

Liu, L., Oza, S., Hogan, D., Perin, J., Rudan, I., Lawn, J.E., Cousens, S., Mathers, C., Black, R.E. (2014). "Global, regional, and national causes of child mortality in 2000-13, with projections to inform post-2015 priorities: an updated systematic analysis." *The Lancet*, vol. 385, No. 9966, pp. 430–440.

Male, Chata and Wodon, Quentin. T. (2016a). Basic profile of child marriage in the Democratic Republic of Congo. Knowledge Brief. Washington, D.C.: World Bank Group. Available from https://openknowledge.worldbank.org/handle/10986/25466.

_____ (2016b). Basic profile of child marriage in Uganda. Knowledge Brief. Washington, D.C.: World Bank Group. Available from http://documents.worldbank.org/curated/en/130701467995446706/Basic-profile-of-child-marriage-in-Uganda.

Mo Ibrahim Foundation (2016). Strength in numbers: Africa's data revolution.

National Bureau of Statistics (2017). Statistical bulletin: monthly tourism 2017/05. Government of Seychelles.

Neumann, B., Vafeidis, T.A., Zimmermann, J. and Nicholls, J.R. (2015). Future coastal population growth and exposure to sea-level rise and coastal flooding: a global assessment. PLoS One, vol. 10, No. 3. Available from www.ncbi.nlm.nih.gov/pmc/articles/PMC4367969/.

National Oceanic and Atmospheric Administration (2013). National coastal population report: trends from 1970 to 2020. Available from http://oceanservice.noaa.gov/facts/coastal-population-report.pdf.

Organization for Economic Cooperation and Development (2010). Measuring aid to agriculture. Available from www.oecd.org/dac/stats/44116307.pdf.

Organization for Economic Cooperation and Development and Paris21 (2013). Strengthening national statistical systems to monitor global goals. Element 5, paper 1.

Paris21 (2017). NSDS guidelines. Available from www.paris21.org/nsdsguidelines.

Robin, N., T. Klein and J. Jutting (2016). Public-private partnerships for statistics: lessons learned, future steps. OECD Development Co-operation Working Paper 27. Paris: Organization for Economic Cooperation and Development.

Safaricom (2016). Annual Report 2016. Nairobi. Available from www.safaricom.co.ke/images/Downloads/Resources_Downloads/Safaricom_Limited_2016_Annual_Report.pdf.

Say, L., Chou, D., Gemmill, A., Tuncalp, O., Moller, A.B., Daniels, J., Gulmezoglu, A.M., Temmerman, M. and Alkema, L. (2014). Global causes of maternal death: a WHO systematic analysis. *The Lancet*, vol. 2, No. 6, pp. e323–e333. Available from www.sciencedirect.com/science/article/pii/S2214109X1470227X.

Shahin, M. (2002). *Hydrology and Water Resources of Africa*. A publication under the Water Science and Technology Library series, vol. 41. New York: Kluwer Academic Publishers.

Singh, S., Darroch, J.E. and Ashford, L.S. (2014). Adding it up: the costs and benefits of investing in sexual and reproductive health 2014. New York: Guttmacher Institute.

Smed, U. T. (2015). Maritime Security and Development in Africa. Centre for Military Studies, University of Copenhagen. Available from cms.polsci.ku.dk/publikationer/maritime-security-and-development-africa/maritim_sikkerhed_og_udvikling_i_afrika__ulrik_trolle_smed_april_2016_.pdf.

Statistics Division (2016). Tier classification for global SDG indicators. New York. Available from https://unstats.un.org/sdgs/files/meetings/iaeg-sdgs-meeting-05/Tier_Classification_of_SDG_Indicators_21_Dec_2016.pdf.

_____ (2017a). UN data: a world of information. Available from http://data.un.org/Data.aspx.

_____ (2017b). SDG indicators: revised list of global Sustainable Development Goal indicators. Available https://unstats.un.org/sdgs/indicators/indicators-list/.

Studies in Poverty and Inequality Institute (2007). The measurement of poverty in South Africa project: key issues. Johannesburg.

Sustainable Development Solutions Network (2015). Data for development: an action plan to finance data revolution for sustainable development.

United Nations, (2015) The Millennium Development Goals Report 2015. Available at: http://www.un.org/millenniumgoals/2015_MDG_Report/pdf/MDG%202015%20rev%20(July%201).pdf

_____ (2016a). The Sustainable Development Goals Report 2016. New York.

_____ (2016b). Report of the Secretary-General: progress towards the Sustainable Development Goals. Available from https://unstats.un.org/sdgs/files/report/2016/secretary-general-sdg-report-2016--EN.pdf.

_____ (2017). Background documents to the Ocean Conference 2017. Available from https://oceanconference.un.org/documents.

United Nations Children's Fund (2016). *The State of the World's Children: A Fair Chance for Every Child*. New York.

_____ (2017). UNICEF data: monitoring the situation of children and women. Available from https://data.unicef.org/topic/maternal-health/maternal-mortality/#.

Walker, T. (2015). When reflecting on maritime security in 2014, there is a good story to tell—but it is not the only one, 6 February. Institute for Security Studies. Available from https://issafrica.org/iss-today/africas-maritime-security-wish-list-for-2015.

World Bank (2016a). *Women, Business and the Law 2016: Getting to Equal*. Washington, D.C.

_____ (2016b). World Bank open data. Available from http://iresearch.worldbank.org/PovcalNet/povOnDemand.aspx.

_____ (2017). World development indicator database. Available from http://databank.worldbank.org/data/reports.aspx?source=world-development-indicators.

World Food Programme (2015). El Niño: implications and scenarios for 2015/16. Available from http://documents.wfp.org/stellent/groups/public/documents/ena/wfp280227.pdf.

World Health Organization (2013). *Women's and Children's Health: Evidence of Impact of Human Rights*. Geneva.

World Health Organization, (2010) World Health Statistics 2010. Available at: http://www.who.int/gho/publications/world_health_statistics/EN_WHS10_Full.pdf

World Health Organization, (2006) Pregnant Adolescents: Delivering in global promises of hope. Available at: http://apps.who.int/iris/bitstream/10665/43368/1/9241593784_eng.pdf

World Trade Organization (2015). Briefing note: agricultural issues. Available from https://www.wto.org/english/thewto_e/minist_e/mc10_e/briefing_notes_e/brief_agriculture_e.htm